PENGUIN BOOKS

Captive

Allan Hall was a New York correspondent for ten years, first for the *Sun* and later for the *Daily Mirror*. He has spent the last fifteen years covering German-speaking Europe for newspapers, including *The Times* and the *Mail on Sunday*. He is the author of some twenty previous books on crime and the paranormal, including the Penguin best-seller *Monster*, an investigation into the life and crimes of Josef Fritzl, and *Girl in the Cellar: The Natascha Kampusch Story*. He lives and works in Berlin.

Captive

*One House, Three Women,
Ten Years in Hell*

ALLAN HALL

PENGUIN BOOKS

PENGUIN BOOKS

Published by the Penguin Group
Penguin Books Ltd, 80 Strand, London WC2R ORL, England
Penguin Group (USA) Inc., 375 Hudson Street, New York, New York 10014, USA
Penguin Group (Canada), 90 Eglinton Avenue East, Suite 700, Toronto, Ontario, Canada M4P 2Y3
(a division of Pearson Penguin Canada Inc.)
Penguin Ireland, 25 St Stephen's Green, Dublin 2, Ireland (a division of Penguin Books Ltd)
Penguin Group (Australia), 707 Collins Street, Melbourne, Victoria 3008, Australia
(a division of Pearson Australia Group Pty Ltd)
Penguin Books India Pvt Ltd, 11 Community Centre, Panchsheel Park, New Delhi – 110 017, India
Penguin Group (NZ), 67 Apollo Drive, Rosedale, Auckland 0632, New Zealand
(a division of Pearson New Zealand Ltd)
Penguin Books (South Africa) (Pty) Ltd, Block D, Rosebank Office Park,
181 Jan Smuts Avenue, Parktown North, Gauteng 2193, South Africa

Penguin Books Ltd, Registered Offices: 80 Strand, London WC2R ORL, England

www.penguin.com

First published 2013
009

Copyright © Allan Hall, 2013

INSET PHOTO CREDITS
All photographs are © Roger Allen except for nos. 28 (© AP Photo/Tony Dejak),
31 (© Matt Sullivan/Getty Images) and 34 (© Cleveland Police/FBI)

Set in 12.5/14.75pt Garamond MT Std
Typeset by Jouve (UK), Milton Keynes
Printed in Great Britain by Clays Ltd, St Ives plc

A CIP catalogue record for this book is available from the British Library

ISBN: 978–0–241–00361–9

www.greenpenguin.co.uk

MIX
Paper from
responsible sources
FSC
www.fsc.org   FSC® C018179

Penguin Books is committed to a sustainable
future for our business, our readers and our planet.
This book is made from Forest Stewardship
Council™ certified paper.

For my wife, Pamela, and Jan-Philipp Litz

Contents

Prologue

On Sundays the bells would peal out, God's ringtone to a material world. They implored those still faithful to attend service, while attempting to convince others that salvation was only feet away for the taking. The chimes echoed in every wooden house on Seymour Avenue in the American city of Cleveland. Only the locals had another, more ironic and half-joking name for the street they lived on – 'See More' Avenue, they called it. See more drugs, see more violence, see more hookers, see more despair, see more trouble. Seymour Avenue was a place on life support a decade ago, and the patient has not made significant progress since. The sound of the bells from the Immanuel Evangelical Lutheran Church on its corner struck chords of hope in an area of chronic social decay and, in one particular house, gave small comfort that God had not forgotten the people who dwelled within its walls.

Perhaps.

House number 2207 Seymour Avenue looked like it might have once featured in an Edward Hopper painting on a lonely prairie. A little worn, a little run-down, but essentially benign. White clapboard walls, wooden front porch, the American eagle symbol of liberty nailed above the deck and a small, tattered Puerto Rican flag hanging limply from a metal holder on one of the wooden beams.

The kind of place where good old boys sip whiskey and smoke cigars on long hot nights. It did not look like a house of horrors, the Gothic monstrosity of Hitchcock's *Psycho*, or the creepy Overlook Hotel of *The Shining* fame. Not even the dark plastic sheeting nailed across the interior windows gave it any particular air of menace. Rather, it seemed as if it had been put there by dilatory painters who had never got around to completing the renovations.

The house was, like the criminal who inhabited it, essentially anonymous. But horrifying crimes took place here. Women stolen from the streets nearby vanished into its maw, there to become the personal sex slaves of the misfit Ariel Castro who, like the house, masked his crimes in plain sight. Women who heard the tolling of the bells but were out of the reach of God's love and protection.

For ten terrible years three unrelated victims – Michelle Knight, Amanda Berry and Gina DeJesus – were degraded, dehumanized and despoiled by a predator with uncontrollable sexual urges who claimed them for his own. Despite neighbours, despite cries for help, despite noises heard by those invited across the threshold by the gatekeeper himself, these young women were lost to an increasingly disconnected world, a world marching to the inexorable drumbeat of 24/7 communications, rolling news, Twitter and Facebook that left no one to wonder what was going on inside 2207 Seymour Avenue.

The women suffered as much from the atomization of society as from the diseased mind of their perverted jailer. A society that, while aware of titanic wars being fought abroad, of drugs destroying their youth, of both adults and children preferring to dwell in a cyber universe of computer games rather than in the real one, looked away from its neighbours as trust evaporated along with feelings of community obligations. The fear of getting involved in something that didn't concern strangers had become entrenched on the street where Castro lived.

Before the three women vanished, Castro had honed his uniquely evil talents on his common-law wife. She inhabited the house of horrors before them, suffered like them, was beaten and humiliated like them in his realm of misery and terror. And, like them, there was no one to step in to save her. Not police, not neighbours, not even her own family. Castro, one of the world's little men, foisted upon Grimilda Figueroa the control he could not exercise upon his own demons. He told her what to eat, who she could befriend, when she could leave the house, when to speak and when to stay silent. He once demanded that she get into a cardboard box and only come out when he said so. He was the lord and master of a fiefdom of pain and misery and, within its narrow borders, he beat her constantly.

She died in 2012, her family insisting it was from the injuries inflicted upon her during Castro's rages. Medical records show she sustained two broken noses, shattered ribs and a blood clot on the brain. She lost a tooth and was permanently hunched from two dislocated shoulders after one particularly horrific frenzy of violence after which she was left dangling in the chains that he would later use on his kidnapped trio.

The first kidnap victim, then 21-year-old Michelle, was

abducted in 2002, followed by then sixteen-year-old Amanda in 2003. Gina was taken in 2004, when she was just fourteen years old. After their dramatic return to the world in May 2013, the girls described a terrifying life where they were controlled both by physical and emotional violence. Though they were not bound when police arrived to take them from the house, they said that in the first few years of their captivity they were often tied with chains that hung from the ceiling of the cellar, from a post in the floor of their rooms, or from heaters on the walls. He raped them repeatedly, and when one of them fell pregnant he punched her time after time in the stomach to induce miscarriages. Only Amanda bore a child who lived – the now six-year-old Jocelyn who, like the others, must climb an Everest of suffering in a bid to reach a worthwhile, endurable life after all the pain.

In the past I have chronicled other monsters of a similar hue, notably the pathetic loner Wolfgang Priklopil, who stole schoolgirl Natascha Kampusch in a desperate bid to make her love him, and Josef Fritzl, who is probably closer to Castro in his modus operandi and his urges. Fritzl earned himself an infamous place in criminal history when he sealed his own daughter up in a DIY dungeon he carved out beneath the family home in Amstetten, Austria, to turn her into his own personal sex toy. Three thousand rapes, twenty-four years and seven children later – six of whom survived – Fritzl was finally brought to justice in a case that stunned the world. No one thought that anything more depraved could ever be visited upon defenceless young women.

And then came along Ariel Castro. In this book all aspects of the horrors endured by the Cleveland captives are explored, while the key figure, Castro, remains centre stage. The world wants to know what made his dark heart beat. What formed him? What motivated him? What petty fortunes of life forced his soul to morph into the twisted, terrible thing it became? From infancy to adulthood, from bus driver by day to rapist and ruler of his home by night, the twisted psyche of Castro is laid bare.

Ultimately, there was a happy ending of sorts. His victims survived. They will heal. They will, it is hoped, find love and happiness in a world they thought had forsaken them. They, not Castro, are the victors.

And how did they come upon their freedom? It was thanks to the little girl, fathered by Castro, who listened to the stories of God's greatness that her mother whispered to her in the darkness. She alone found the courage to save them all.

1. Such a Nice Guy

Duey is the kind of place young men – and monsters – dream about leaving.

The lush coffee fields of Puerto Rico present an inviting vista to tourists, but for the impoverished local people they signify nothing but back-breaking work, day in, day out, for a pittance. The sun shines down relentlessly, driving the temperature and humidity level ever higher. Close to 50 per cent of the people in the Yauco district, where the hamlet of Duey lies, live below the poverty line and have very little hope of ever crossing it. *La Isla del Encanto* – 'the Enchanted Isle' – is the name generations of proud Puerto Ricans have given to their birthplace. To the poor people of Duey, it is often referred to as *La Tierra de los Condenados* – 'the Land of the Damned'.

When the burning sun dips down over the shimmering Caribbean sea, many people who give their heart to Jesus, by day, offer it to the Santeria gods, at night. Santeria is a kind of voodoo-lite, but one which still involves animal sacrifices and idolatry of strange and terrifying deities, inviting condemnation from mainstream clerics and accusations that it is the source of brainwashing and fanaticism. It is, in itself, a form of escape for those who physically cannot leave.

It is no surprise that generations of Puerto Ricans have looked northwards to America for salvation, both from the poverty and the pressures of the Santeria priests. Classified as an 'unincorporated territory of the USA', this island is virtually a state of its mighty neighbour. It has the dollar for its currency, American TV, movies and products for its culture, and citizenship of the USA is an automatic right for all inhabitants. America has beckoned the natives to leave ever since the promise of betterment and the pursuit of happiness offered a way out and up. It was a siren call that would have been heard in Duey, 1,839 miles from the northern US city of Ohio, and would have resonated with a young man called Ariel Castro, had he been old enough to recognize what it offered. Born on 10 July 1960 at the Hospital Metropolitano Dr Tito Mattei in Yauco, he came into the world with prospects seemingly lower than the roots of the coffee plants that would, in all probability, have been his to attend to later in life. He was a middle child in a family of four – his brother Onil was born two years before him and his brother Pedro two years afterwards, and there was an elder sister, Marisol Alicea. Childhood was spent in scrubby streets, playing on tinder-dry grass, emulating basketball and baseball stars from far away with little hope of ever joining his heroes. His talent, such as it was, lay in music; family members said he liked percussion instruments as a child but longed for a 'big, shiny guitar' of the sort he would come to master as a teenager in America. In Puerto Rico he attended state schools, like thousands of others, where he displayed mediocre intelligence and little enthusiasm for academia.

He seems to have had an unremarkable childhood until he suffered the seismic emotional shock, at the age of ten, of his parents' separation. His father, Pedro, had left the family in 1954 to head for America, where he opened a used-car lot in Cleveland, returning infrequently.

And when he did, there was usually trouble.

Poverty, drink and domestic violence – the toxic trinity which harms so many innocent children and prepares them to imitate their parents' behaviour when they grow up – drove apart Lillian and Pedro Castro, a parting which is still a source of some shame to relatives of the Castro clan living in Puerto Rico. Lillian had had enough of poverty and abuse and made her decision to get to America too, to stake her claim for a better life for herself and her children before it was too late. She was sickened by the violence that swirled around her husband – he had lost an arm to a machete blow as a young man in a dispute with local gangsters – and she did not want the same fate to befall her sons. Pedro Castro maintained contact with his wife when she went to the USA, but he took no further role in family life.

Lillian took with her the secrets of a frightened young Ariel who, years later, would claim he had been routinely sexually abused by his father's brother as a child. Was it true? Abuse there certainly was. But the uncle in question is no longer around to deny it, and Ariel proved he was an Olympic-class liar during the ten years he lived with his secret captives. It was, however, a mantra he chanted continuously after his arrest and one for the mind doctors to toy with as the search for the catalyst of his unique catalogue of cruelties continues. Abuse takes many forms, and one thing seems certain: Ariel Castro displayed all the traits of having been a victim before he became the abuser.

The relatives in Duey believe it was the act of his parents' divorce itself which triggered the boy's descent into depravity. 'Maybe that's what messed up Ariel,' said Hilberto Caraballo, aged seventy-six, who knew the parents. 'When you are crazy, you need any excuse, I guess. I know some folks talk about drink and stuff, but Pedro was a good dad to Ariel before the break-up.'

His cousin Javier Castro, aged forty-eight, nodded his head in agreement, saying, 'Most of us are good here. I have two sons aged fifteen and twenty-three. One person can't shame an entire family. We won't let it. But I wish we could say now we weren't cousins. I don't feel comfortable being associated with him – we are good people, even if he is evil. We don't know what kind of demon he had in him to do what he did. A demon inside him made him lose his mind.'

Lillian took Ariel, together with her three other children, to settle initially in the city of Reading, Pennsylvania, where two of her sisters and her own mother were already living. The boy was close to his mother and a favourite of hers. He was quiet, introverted, someone she needed to hug close to her at night when he came home from school in tears because the local children had insulted him as a 'Rican', a 'spic', a 'wetback'. Now aged seventy-five, Mrs Castro is still admired by all the Castro clan, both in America and back on the Enchanted Isle. 'She is the rock of the family, and she's always been there for whoever needs her,' said a woman who is one of dozens of Ariel Castro's relatives in Berks County, Pennsylvania.

At the time, Lillian and her children lived with relatives from a branch of the family by the name of Rodriguez, at 435 North Second Street in Reading, and the Castro children attended Lauer's Park Elementary School. City records show that the uprooted, now fatherless, group were there during 1970 and 1971. 'Every single day out here, on the street, all the kids played together. We played kick the can when there were still bricks here on the sidewalk,' said Joe Gonzalez, whose grandmother lived directly across the street from the Castro family.

Another neighbour said, 'The mother was a family woman through and through, so there must have been a hell of a good reason for her to break up the home and schlep all the way to America. The scuttlebutt around here was that Pedro got a bit loose with his fists when he was on the rum. And he was apparently on the rum a lot. Even when she moved away to Cleveland, Lillian brought the kids back every year, made sure the bonds with the Rodriguezes were intact, seeing all her nieces and nephews. She is a good woman. Sometimes she would stay for months at a time.'

Lillian made sure she brought her children back from Cleveland for their grandmother's funeral when the old lady died in the late 1970s.

The enormity of what Ariel Castro the man has done is incomprehensible to the Castro tribe, most of whom have frozen him in their memories as a child. Lillian Castro still has two sisters and a brother in Reading. 'My dad wants to stress that Lillian didn't raise Ariel this way,' said one of those siblings. The woman said she remembers Ariel as a normal child. As an adult, he talked to her occasionally on the phone. He would always tell her he missed her and asked when she was coming to visit him. The last time they spoke was about a year and a half ago. As always, he seemed 'normal and happy. Nothing seemed strange.' But then, after his maniacal scheme finally unravelled, the family learned that he was a master of projecting banality when evil pulsated at his very core.

'The only red flag for Lillian Castro, the only one, is that Ariel never invited her into his home,' the cousin said. 'This was kinda strange for a guy who was so close to his mom. Instead, he'd always go to her house for dinner, or tell her to leave her home-cooked meals on his porch. But she thought that was because he was a hoarder, and she had no clue what was really happening inside.'

'It's indescribable what she is going through, what the rest of the family is going through,' said one of her nieces, who describes Lillian as being like a mother to her. 'I spoke to her a little bit after the news broke about what they had found in his house, and she doesn't sound like herself. She said it's hard to believe your flesh and blood did something like this.'

Cleveland, where Lillian moved her family in 1974, was once the industrial jewel in America's crown. It grew rich from supplying the materiel necessary for the North to defeat the South in the Civil War, and with wealth came grand houses, statement skyscrapers, fine civic parks and elegant boulevards. Steel, coal, cars – all these heavy industries went on to thrive in Cleveland, which was once the sixth-largest city in the United States. The forebears of Lillian Castro worked in those steel mills and automobile plants, with some members catching the American can-do spirit early on, investing in rental properties and opening small businesses on the lower west side (some of which are still operating today).

'They are very industrious and business-minded people,' said Adrian Maldonado, aged fifty-three, who runs a construction consulting company and grew up in the area around West 25th Street and Clark Avenue, where many Castros settled. 'The Castro clan is a big clan, so you'll always have a couple of rotten apples.'

According to Maldonado and former Cleveland Councilman Nelson Cintron Jr., the Castros have widespread business ties. Julio 'Cesi' Castro, now aged seventy-eight, arrived from Duey in the early 1950s and opened a typical mom-and-pop bodega, Caribe Grocery, on West 25th Street. He runs it to this day. The late Pedro 'Nano' Castro, Ariel's father, purchased a used-car lot at West 25th Street and Sacket Avenue. An uncle of Ariel's is remembered as the first Latino record shop owner in Cleveland, back in the 1970s, on West 25th Street. Norbert 'Berto' Castro, a cousin, still owns a hardware store on Clark Avenue.

'There isn't anybody in the neighbourhood who doesn't know Cesi,' said Maldonado, speaking of the patriarch of the Castro clan. 'If you were short on your rent, you went to Cesi and said, "Hey, could you lend me $50?" He always gave you money. And if you needed milk or bread and were short on cash, he'd always give you credit.'

José Feliciano, a lawyer and head of the Hispanic Roundtable, a civic group working to empower Latinos, echoed Maldonado's praise of Cesi Castro. 'He's helped more Hispanic families than the entire welfare department,' he said. 'He's an extraordinary human being.'

Cesi Castro says Ariel was his 'special nephew, the one with the smarts. There are very few people who can teach themselves how to play the bass. But now I see that, apparently, he was living two personalities. The personality that I saw was the personality that was dealing with kids and driving the bus, the personality of being a musician and playing the bass. Now I know there was another and it pains me, pains everyone who knew him. How could he do it?'

Castro success stories apart, Cleveland, like all big cities, has seen its own reverse in life's fortunes. Poverty has surged in recent years as the riches garnered by entrepreneurs and inventors in the earlier part of the last century have become a distant memory. Ghettos and seedy neighbourhoods, the archetypal wrong-side-of-the-tracks settlements, abound, the most recent ones brought low by an explosion in drugs (first crack cocaine, later crystal meth). The city's Puerto Rican population ballooned after the Second World War, and Castro relatives were among the first settlers on the west side of the city – the place where Ariel lived, and where his criminality festered unseen.

While there have been undoubted civic achievements among the Latino community, Ariel Castro's neighbourhood is, by and large, an area of profound underachievement.

The escape by Amanda Berry, Gina DeJesus and Michelle Knight from Castro's house in May 2013 focused an unwelcome spotlight on the city's Latino community. Parts of it suffer from devastating poverty, with a median income for families of four below $15,000 annually (more than $8,000 below what government agencies say is the survival line). One in five homes is vacant – the knock-on effect of the sub-prime mortgage crisis of 2007–2008 which contributed to the slide in poor neighbourhoods when tenants found they could no longer pay the rent and owners couldn't afford the mortgage. About 7 out of 10 Puerto Rican children fail to graduate from high school, while the overall pass rate is about 65 per cent. Criminality – the lure of big money from drugs, protection rackets or illicit gambling – thrives as a result.

It also thrived in parts of the extended family of the Castros. In 1971, before Ariel arrived in Cleveland, FBI agents seized large quantities of cash, gambling records and guns from eleven people including Cesi Castro, Berto and Pedro, during a raid on Cesi's bodega. Although no arrests were made, the Castros were dragged into a wider probe by the Feds aimed at a game called Bolita.

'That was a big thing back in the day, the numbers racket,' said Maldonado. 'Now it's the Ohio Lottery, which is easier and cleaner.'

But back when Lillian and the Castro brothers arrived, there was no lottery. The numbers racket was something that youngsters learned from an early age in neighbourhoods where every household flew the Puerto Rican flag, instead of the Stars and Stripes, and where Spanish was the mother tongue of the home, the streets and the bars. There was such a concentration of people from Yauco in the neighbourhood Lillian moved into that a social club called 'The Spirit of Yauco' was a focal point for the community. The local park was named for the Puerto Rican baseball star Roberto Clemente, and a school took the name of Luis Muñoz Marín, the political legend often referred to as the 'Father of Modern Puerto Rico'.

Ariel Castro graduated from Lincoln West High School in 1979, aged eighteen, and was true to the unfortunate Puerto Rican stereotype. He had few academic qualifications, equalling few prospects outside of dishwashing, labouring or waiting tables. He wasn't backward at school – far from it, he excelled in music and mathematics, English and Spanish – but he was easily satisfied, lazy, convinced that life's glittering prizes would fall into his lap. His mother was warned a year before he left that his final grades were heading south, but there was little discipline in the household. Although his father had now moved to Cleveland, he was not involved to any great extent in the young man's upbringing. Castro Jr. was allowed to drift; he could bend his mother to his will, and there was no one to give him the hard word, the masculine discipline, when he most needed it.

He knew the sheer numbers of Castro clan members in the city meant that there was a ready supply of cheap loans available when he left school. He and his brothers tried their hands running several small businesses, including a grocery store and a garage, but Ariel drifted back into more menial work. He was employed, at various times, working on the checkout bagging groceries at a Pick-N-Pay supermarket, at the Lesner Products on Columbus Road as a drill press operator, and at Curnba Motors as a helper and driver. After his father's death, in 1984, court records show that he picked up just over $11,000 in his will. Music, however, was his first love and remained so. He was attracted to the Hispanic bars and clubs, which were always good for a night's pay for decent musicians. As a teenager, Ariel Castro mastered the 'plena', a folkloric style of Puerto Rican music. But he could do it all: salsa, merengue, jazz. According to a man who performed with him at cultural events in the 1990s, he evolved into one of the top three Latin bass players in the city.

'Definitely a pro,' recalls Alberto Fermin, who played in a band with Castro for two years. 'It wasn't just a hobby. Castro may have worked factory jobs, but he also saw music as a way to make extra income.'

The music may have put extra dollars in his pocket but it was doing nothing to soothe his tormented psyche. He was growing more embittered with each passing day, though he didn't show it.

Yet.

The face he presented to the world was one of affability, conformity, normality. Only within did he seethe.

Thousands of miles away from Cleveland, on a continent Castro never visited and will now never see, a man called Josef Fritzl was also a master of disguise. Fritzl has gone down in criminal history as the sexually obsessed father who would tolerate no dissent in his family, whose driving need for absolute control extended over every single one of his children and his wife. His wilful daughter Elisabeth refused to bend to his wishes and so, with a rape conviction behind him and a prison term that he didn't want to repeat, but cursed with an insatiable libido, he drugged her and walled her up in a secret underground cellar that became her personal rape hell for twenty-four long years.

Fritzl and Castro are polar opposites in many ways, and mirror images in others. At their twisted cores both believed in the righteousness of their berserk callings. They saw women as nothing but bitches and whores, to be used by masterful beings like themselves who know best, who know what women *really* want, not what they say they want. Both had a fixation for their own mothers, putting them on a pedestal to which the sluts and tramps, in their mangled reasoning, would never, could never, ascend. And both had the cunning to fool sophisticated western societies into thinking they were on the level.

What drove them, most experts believe, is simple enough: power. 'To kidnap and control someone for an extended period is to exert influence over another person that few can imagine,' said one psychologist. 'But that is something that these men – and they are almost always men – crave. Castro seems to fit that bill.'

Patricia Saunders PhD, a New York-based clinical and forensic psychologist, said in an interview for this book that sexual abuse, coupled with the trauma of his parents' divorce, could indeed have been the catalyst for Ariel Castro's world view, culminating in his terrible crimes. 'If he was sexually abused as a child, his behaviour would be a matter of feeling mastery over a situation. Castro wanted complete and utter control over these three girls. It is the identification of an aggressor. The person will do something to others that happened to themselves in order to master it. It is a very clearly patterned series of behaviours that went on for a very long time. I think it will prove to be significant that he chose to have a baby with the girl Amanda, the middle one in terms of age, while beating the older one into miscarriages. His fantasy may have been that he was unconsciously trying to re-birth himself. He was the middle child in his own family and perhaps it was significant for him, for reasons only he knows, to continue this lineage with the captive who was in the middle, age-wise – like he was, growing up.

'Children are deeply traumatized by divorce. They don't just feel abandoned. They feel that everything has been taken from them. Castro took everything from these girls in return. It appears this man is a psychopath. He had no capacity for empathy. The man had no conscience, despite knowing what he was doing was wrong, which is the classic hallmark of a psychopath. Sadly, there are a hell of a lot more of them out there than you would think.

'He probably wasn't exorcizing his demons with his treatment of his captives. For a psychopath there are no demons. They *are* the demons. There are no conflicts, no conscience. They are trying to undo their own traumas by being the abuser. It revolves around power and control. Psychopaths know that by society's standards what they are doing is wrong, but they don't care. They don't have attachments to other human beings. Other human beings are just objects to service their needs.

'Cases like the Cleveland long-time abductions are rare, shocking and raise many questions. They also fascinate us because we can't "get it", we don't understand why someone would commit such acts. There is some research literature on kidnappers and abductions, but little or no empirical studies that can really give us clear answers. I think that neglect, his neglect as a child, most definitely played a psychological role – they might have felt like objects, things for their parents' use. There are psychological parallels in aggressive, dominant rapists, paedophiles and sadistic killers, where the predominant theme is power and control over the victims. Some researchers believe that this dimension adds secondary pleasure to the sexual assaults and, clearly, the act of keeping women as slaves speaks to domination as an overriding need.

'The Cleveland victims were adolescents when they were initially kidnapped and enslaved, which may have had an element of paedophilia in it. However, as these women were kept as "slaves", the theme changed to power and control. A more subtle psychological element is that Castro may have felt entitled to his acts for a variety of reasons: life had been unfair to him so "they deserve this"; a complete lack of empathy for the victims, families and community; and a personality structure where fantasies and sexual and aggressive impulses overrode any normal inhibition.

'Current empirical research on serial sexual homicides suggests such offenders have very clear and detailed fantasies or "scripts" in their heads, which they yearn to act on.

The constellation of anger, poor impulse control, lack of conscience, and opportunity allows them to act on these scripts and play them out in real life. Such men often have histories of previous crimes of domestic violence, sexual assaults and stalking. Men like Castro are developmentally arrested and perhaps just very different than the average human being. Some psychologists have gone as far as saying that psychopaths are an evolutionary offshoot of human beings; that is, they are fundamentally a different kind of homo sapiens and we know that psychotherapy and medication rarely change their behaviour. It is in them.'

Castro masked his inner gnawing, his nascent dark side, as a young man – just as Fritzl and Priklopil (the kidnapper of Natascha Kampusch in 1998), masked theirs as mature, solid, patriarchal figures.

Awkward with girls he met at the obligatory Friday night drinkathons at venues such as Club Paraiso, Castro emanated a faux-friendly, masculine clubbiness to the outside world that was in stark contrast to the maelstrom of angry, impotent rage he felt within. A former pal who did not want to be identified in full as someone who used to hang out with him, remembers an incident on a Saturday night when both men were in their early twenties.

'We would sometimes meet and have a few brews and then go girl hunting,' said Don. 'I knew him from school. We weren't best buddies but we collided from time to time, sometimes in a group, sometimes just ourselves. On this one night the other guys peeled off and we ended up at the Lido on West 117th Street. It's kinda a timewarped place where the clock stopped around 1974 and never got rebooted. But there were always lots of guys and lots of girls, all doing the mating thing, you know, and the odd stripper dance. Ariel was always a little weird about going there, like he was uncomfortable or something. He wasn't good around girls, awkward, a little shy.

'On this night we got to talking with a couple of sweet-looking *chiquitas*, you know, nicely dressed in figure-hugging skirts and high heels. There was a brunette who was talking to Ariel and I was jawing with her pal, a redhead. Things seemed to be going OK. Then the girls say they're doing the ladies-room thing, and I turn to Ariel and say something like, "Looks like a homer tonight!" And he puts his drink down and starts to walk away. I grab him and ask what's going on and he says, "They're sluts, Don, don't you see that? Little whores with too much make-up. I'm going home." I thought he was kidding. What, he wanted to go out with a nun or something? I was really embarrassed, man, you know. These girls came back from the powder room and I had to say he was sick, that he had gone home.

'I saw him again a couple of days later, and he never mentioned it. And I didn't either. But I didn't go out with him after that. I mean, he was totally wrong. They were really nice girls – and he would have gone home alone, anyway, without the drama show.'

This description, this utter contempt for females, surfaced time and time again in Ariel Castro. It was witnessed at first hand by a man who came to know him well, who visited his Seymour Avenue home during the time it served as a dungeon and who, like everyone else, had no real idea about the dark side of the man he called a friend. Santos 'Tito' DeJesus – an uncle to the girl Gina who would later become one of his friend's captives – said to the author of this book, 'He was a great band player but a loser with women. He displayed a contempt for them that was sometimes frightening. I knew him for twenty years and, like, if a girl refused to dance with him he would go off on one. He would go back time after time after time to ask her, and when she said no again he would walk back spitting insults – "bitch", "whore", that kind of thing. I used to say to him, "Leave it, man, you're embarrassing yourself. The girl don't want to dance with you, go ask someone else. Don't get all worked up about it." But he wouldn't take no for an answer.'

Doctors recognize this as classic psychopathic behaviour: doing the same thing over and over again, while always expecting a different outcome.

Tito went on: 'I think, at the very heart of things, he was a loner. We went on the road to places like Pittsburgh and Cincinnati, but he never had a girlfriend in tow like some of the guys. I think he also had a very arrogant streak in him. Sometimes, when we were setting things up on stage, he would arrange it so that he took the prime spot, which wasn't his, you know, because he was playing bass. It was like he had low self-esteem or something. There was a lot of anger in him – a lot, all bottled up – and sometimes I would witness it. He would be bitching about this and that, I would tell him to chill, and he would say, "F**k you, you're an idiot," and I would tell him to take his anger out on stage, not on me. I guess if you add it all up, he was a small guy who had real issues. I would never have guessed that they would drive him to do what he did. But, you know, I think, looking back on it now, I think perhaps he was capable of anything.'

William Perez, aged seventy, owns the Belinda nightclub in the heartland of the Hispanic community in Cleveland. It is a cavern of a place that resembles a factory from the outside but has a shining ballroom-sized interior adjacent to a bar. William, a jovial and open man, has known Ariel Castro almost all of his life. He knew the family back in Puerto Rico, and he hosted the bands in which Ariel played. He wears the look of a man who has been conned, as he freely admits he has been.

'Yep,' he said to the author. 'I guess you could say he conned us all. I keep on reading how people keep on saying the same things as I do about him: nice guy, regular, talented in music. But I have had time to reflect in the weeks since those girls were rescued, and I guess you could say there were things about him that made me uneasy. I drank back then, so I suppose I forgot about them, but he was definitely weird in some departments. I remember, in particular, one time when he wanted to use my van to haul some equipment from his home to the club. It was snowing outside and inside it was wet and messy. He made a real scene about it, bitching and moaning and getting really angry that it was not in a fit state. I told him it was that or carrying the stuff through the drifts. But that intense anger . . . man, I have to say, it scared me.

'His talent as a musician saved him, I guess, from being totally cut off from everyone. Always a bit of a loner, the music made him liked and gave him some confidence – the confidence which he definitely didn't have with women. As far as I knew him, he liked cars and music and was frustrated that he wasn't more successful with girls. He was a guy I knew, who I never really knew. What can I say?'

Castro's lack of self-esteem also displayed itself in fantasies – another trait common in psychopaths. Ian Brady, a serial killer of little boys and girls in England in the 1960s, pretended he was a Nazi spy during his killing spree, projecting images on to the canvas of his mind, an 'us-and-them' melodrama, one man against the world. Castro, too, had his little dramas to spice up what was turning into a less than stellar life. One childhood friend of Castro's recalled how a music session with him suddenly turned bizarre.

'Ariel was in my garage, probably five or six years ago. We were recording a song, an idea we had – a little hard rock with some Latin,' said Joe Popow, aged forty-five, a father of six who has known the Castro brothers since childhood. 'And – you're going to laugh – he said he was in the CIA. And I don't know if he was joking or not, but it's the way he said it, how serious he said it. I didn't know what he was capable of. That just put me on the defensive, and I just started stepping away.'

His brother Onil – who, along with Pedro, was considered an accomplice in Ariel Castro's crimes until police realized he had fooled them, as he had fooled everyone else – spoke of the 'apartness' of their sibling while they grew. 'Yeah, he was a little apart from us all, strange to me through all of our lives. He always stayed to himself with his music. When he moved out there would be times when we wouldn't see him for a month, two weeks. Mama used to say after he moved into his house, "Check your brother, check on your brother. He lives alone in that house. He's a loner. You don't know if he's OK or what's going on." So I would text him and he would text me back. "What are you doing?" "I'm fine." And that was it. That was our relationship.'

In February 1991, with a slew of low-grade, low-paid jobs behind him, Ariel Castro went to work for the Cleveland Metropolitan School District as a bus driver. In his application for the job, he wrote: 'I enjoy working with children. I have a good driving record. I speak English and Spanish. I plan to drive a bus and working [*sic*] with young people.' He was paid $12.33 an hour for driving the bus, which gave him a wage, without stoppages and overtime, of under $555 a week. Although he outwardly connected with the children that he drove to and from a variety of local schools, his bonhomie and apparent concern for his charges was ultimately a charade. Darlene Dos Reis, a work colleague, said she did not like working with him: 'I found him to be very mean and hateful with the children. It was like he hated them really, even though he smiled at them.'

Castro underwent just the briefest of vettings to get the job. Although he held it down for twenty-two years – including all the years during which his fiendish scheme at Seymour Avenue was playing out – he made several mistakes which testified to his character before he was eventually dismissed. He once made an illegal U-turn in the bus in rush-hour traffic; he once used the vehicle in between school runs to do his home shopping; and he once left a special-needs student alone on the bus while he ate his lunch in a Wendy's fast-food outlet. On that occasion he is alleged to have referred to the male student using the epithet he most liked to apply to women: 'bitch'. He also ignored a fight among students on the bus, which resulted in several bloody noses. He was eventually given the sack for parking the bus, unattended, for four hours outside a school, blocking the fire lane reserved for emergency vehicles.

Despite all the times when he was reckless and feckless, he still maintained the confidence of the local headteachers whose pupils he drove. One even wrote a formal letter of support after the incident with the special-needs student, stating that Castro had his full support because, 'I have witnessed him trying to work with students, families and myself to handle student issues.'

Most of the people who dealt with him seemed to give Ariel Castro the benefit of the doubt, becoming unwitting enablers to his later crimes.

In 1992, Castro bought the house on Seymour Avenue, number 2207, right in the heart of the Puerto Rican community. A white clapboard affair with a small front yard and an extensive area at the back, the house lay in what is now a decaying zone of family homes – although it wasn't exactly Beverly Hills when he bought it. Squeezed in between the Interstate 90 freeway and Scranton Cemetery, most of the houses give out an aura of neglect. Their residents appear to be sliding into a poverty that is reflected in the peeling and chipped facades of the houses. Drug dealers once flourished in these streets, but they too have moved on to more profitable pitches. The houses sport 'Beware of the Dog' signs and 'Keep Out!' notices in bold red letters. The block is anchored at its eastern end by the stately red-brick Immanuel Evangelical Lutheran Church. At the west end, across West 25th Street, is the well-known Caribe Grocery, owned by Uncle Cesi.

During the years he was the master at number 2207, Castro flew the Puerto Rican flag from the porch where he often sat in the evening consuming hamburgers, fries and other fast-food takeaways from large brown paper bags, occasionally breaking off bits of burger bun to feed to the red cardinal birds which visited in springtime. He liked a beer too but was not, according to those who knew him well, a drinker on anything like the epic scale of his brothers.

Ariel's home, a four-bedroom, one-bathroom affair, cost him $12,000. Local records show that the sale went through on 29 April that year, from Edwin and Antonia Castro. It is unclear if they are relatives or just bear the same name. At the time of his arrest Cuyahoga County Auditor's records showed that the two-storey house, complete with basement, was valued at $36,100. County records indicated Castro owed $2,501.01 in back taxes in May 2013 and had last paid real-estate taxes in 2010. The house had been flagged for foreclosure, but court records show no indication that the county government had foreclosed.

When he first moved in, he turned one room of the house into a music room. But he didn't welcome fellow musicians – or, indeed, any visitors. Neighbours couldn't help but notice that, in a community where the back door was often left open for residents to pop in and out of one another's homes, Ariel never allowed anyone to cross the threshold. It did not diminish his nice-guy disguise, but it was noted.

Sadly, later, it was never acted upon.

One trait of Castro's that all commented upon, friends and enemies alike, was his chronic inability to be anywhere on time. He was often reprimanded by his bus company superiors for being late for his shifts, although it was never deemed serious enough for disciplinary warnings.

'The only thing – and I mean the only thing – I remember about him was that he was always late to practice,' said Miguel Quinones, manager of Grupo Fuego, which has played in north-east Ohio since 1999.

Castro played with the Latin band in 2008. The band never practised at Castro's home, and none of the band members were ever invited for a visit.

'The band rehearsed at the musical director's place,' added Quinones. 'We stopped working with Castro because he was always late. He only played two gigs with Grupo Fuego, one in Youngstown and another in Cleveland, before being fired.'

Castro also played bass, on and off, for fifteen years in Grupo Kanon, which is widely known in Cleveland's Hispanic community for its performances at clubs, churches and cultural celebrations. Band leader Ivan Ruiz knew Castro for about twenty years but never saw him with another person – woman or man – even though he appeared in various groups, playing his bass.

'He could do the job, but he became increasingly defensive and unreliable over the years,' said Ruiz. 'It was like he couldn't leave his house.'

No one could figure out why.

Castro did invite Ruiz' seventeen-year-old son over once, to have him rehearse the drums. Automatically, Ruiz answered, 'No, don't go.' A restaurateur and long-time Clevelander, Ruiz is known on the local music scene as 'Popo'. He recalled, 'I didn't trust having him with my child. There was just something about him that sent up this warning flare. He was a senile kind of person, a crazy kind of person, he was weird. He was always late for gigs and rehearsals. He always had to leave at the earliest moment too. I fired him last year.'

Ruiz and others recalled that Castro always had a set of excuses on hand for his tardiness.

'Traffic or running late,' said Quinones. 'Excuses a musician might make up. He was just too unreliable.'

Other bands Castro played with include Los Boy'z Del Merengue, who have had gigs at places such as Belinda's. He also performed with renowned local band leader Roberto Ocasio, in 2003. But mostly, aside from timekeeping, the people he mixed with just regarded him as anonymous – a nice, regular guy. This was the descriptive phrase that was most often used to define the monster in their midst.

Juan Perez, aged twenty-seven, lived two houses along from Castro. 'He was a fun guy,' he recalled. 'I mean, parents trusted him. He talked to the parents, took an interest in the kids. He was just a regular guy on the street. He put on that great mask that everyone thought he was a good guy. I guess around here we thought he was a charismatic guy. He always took time out to play with the kids in the neighbourhood, often riding his bicycle around, offering them rides up and down the block. We thought he was a great guy. Nice guy. Perfect gentleman. The mask he had on was amazing. My parents trusted him enough to let me play with his kids. Real cool guy. Helped me with a flat tyre once. He was just really nice.'

Baptist preacher Dr Mark Rosset of Marion, Virginia, said it was Castro's ability to project an image of harmlessness that served him so well in the perpetration of his lengthy crimes. 'To most people, Ariel Castro did not look like a monster. His friends said about him that he was a nice man, he was polite, a cool bass player, and a sweet, happy person. Castro was a school bus driver. He had children and grandchildren. He would have dinner at his mother's house, with his brothers. Castro knew the families of his victims, even attending vigils for the missing girls. There, he prayed for the same girls whom he had earlier preyed upon.

'He was a monster in sheep's clothing. Monsters do not start out big. Maybe, they begin as nine-year-old little monsters who never learn about respect or human dignity. Little monsters become big monsters, and a monster is a monster. That is what Castro became.'

Perez added that Castro was not deemed weird or awkward in the neighbourhood – rather, his easy charm with the local children made him a popular man. Often, when riding his bicycle, or a four-wheeler, he would give kids rides up and down the block.

This portrait was backed up by other neighbours who never saw beyond the mask. But why should they?

If Ariel Castro's neighbours had been able to peek into the secret hiding places of his house in the pre-internet days, they would have seen the stocks of hardcore pornography he stashed away there.

Much of it involved pain, some of it involved children, and none of it was of the *Playboy* or *Penthouse* variety. It was lurid, vile, obscene stuff. Later, much later, equally disturbing images were found on his computer after his demented mission was finally brought to an end, images which gave an insight into the world of fantasy that he had brought to life. In this he shared another common trait with the lustful Fritzl in Austria.

Shortly after Fritzl incarcerated his daughter in the secret dungeon beneath his home, he visited her clutching a variety of grotesquely large sex toys and piles of magazines. She testified at his trial that she was forced to emulate the acts in the pornographic pictures, time after terrible time, until he had violated her and fathered seven children with her, six of whom survived.

'Pornography is the theory; rape is the practice,' wrote feminist author Robin Morgan. For Ariel Castro the maxim held true. On his computer police found evidence of Castro's visits to numerous websites where women were sexually humiliated, beaten, raped.

Feminist researcher Gail Dines has said, 'We are now

bringing up a generation of boys on cruel, violent porn. And given what we know about how images affect people, this is going to have a profound influence on their sexuality, behaviour and attitudes towards women. Pornography can have a driving effect on men to commit acts of violence against women. I am clear that this does *not* mean, as critics sometimes suggest, that all men who look at porn will go on to rape. But I posit that porn gives permission to its consumers to treat women as they are treated in porn.'

During the times before Castro settled down with his first real victim – Grimilda Figueroa, his long-suffering common-law wife – there are many instances of his contemptuous attitude towards women. Some of his neighbours recognized this contempt for women. Doug Parker, owner of the house next door to Castro's and who lived in it for a while before turning it into a rental property, described his next-door neighbour as a 'real nut job'.

Parker said, 'We are arch enemies, I can't disguise that. He needs to dominate and he does it underhandedly because he can't do it like a man. There's something missing in the guy's make-up. He once took the trash cans from the back of the house and told me I needed to wash them – this after I had been there just three days. It was the start of years of bad blood. One time I was out at work and I came home to find my wife in tears. I asked her what had happened and she said he had been on the porch, calling her a bitch, a slut. Well, that was it. That was assault, good as, for me. I grabbed my gun I keep for protection in this neighbourhood and knocked on his door brandishing it.

'I am not exactly proud of how I handled it. I told him

if he ever talked to her again, we were going to have big problems. "You mess with my family!" I said to him, shaking the gun at him. He never talked to her again. The whole time I was living next door to him the house was a locked-down place. When you knocked on the door, you'd hear "click, click, click", the series of locks being undone. He's always been like that. After I moved out, I would come over in summer when the tenant wanted something doing or to tidy up. Summer heat in Cleveland is a killer but there was no A/C running in his house and all the blinds were tightly shut, not a window was open. And I knew Castro was inside the house, because the car was parked out front. Now I know why he kept it so buttoned down. But I never knew what was happening inside there. Who could?'

Occasionally, neighbours would see the Castro brothers visit Ariel at his run-down Fort Knox. Pedro and Onil were, according to those who knew them, in a state of almost perpetual drunkenness and out of work for most of their lives. While his brothers got around town on bicycles, Ariel owned four motorcycles and several cars, including a Jeep Cherokee and a red Toyota pickup. He didn't drink nearly as much as his brothers, but neither was he teetotal.

Pedro and Onil lived on Kinkel Street with their mother, Pedro subsisting on social security handouts and Onil on disability payments. No one ever saw Onil and Pedro with female companions; they were in thrall to their mother, who had become a devout Jehovah's Witness during her time in America. She was a matriarch who, nevertheless, was banned from stepping over the threshold of what was to become anything but an ordinary home in the hands of Ariel Castro.

A friend of Lillian's said, 'Like all mothers she could see no bad and no harm in her children. Ariel she always had a soft spot for. But she was upset that she had to, as she said to me, "make an appointment to see my own son. Isn't that just a little extreme?" She didn't know the half of it. But then, neither did any of us.'

Before news broke of Ariel Castro's crimes, the Castro family was essentially seen as flawed but harmless. 'They were always drinking,' said a neighbour of Pedro and Onil's. 'Anything. Liquor, or beer. They drank a lot.'

A long-time friend of the brothers, Nelson Roman, said both Pedro and Onil ruined their health and employment prospects with alcohol. 'But they were all good kids. That's why this news is devastating. It's not only horrifying to the families of the kidnapped girls, it's devastating to us, because these brothers grew up in a good family.'

Samira Abdul Karim, a friend of Lillian's for thirty years, added, 'Even if they are drunk all the time, they're nice. They would come to my house and sit outside with me and talk. And even when they were drunk, they had a sense of humour. They laughed all the time.'

City records show the brothers also had routine run-ins with the law for minor infractions such as drunkenness. Pedro has had ten cases filed against him since 1994. Onil has had four. None were more serious than a misdemeanour.

*

Cruelty develops at different tempos in different monsters. Ian Brady, the notorious child killer who stalked
young children in the north of England in the 1960s
before raping and killing them, then interring them in
unmarked graves on the lonely moors around the city of
Manchester, nurtured his hideous side by burying cats
alive before he was in his teens. Serial killer and cannibal
Jeffrey Dahmer, imprisoned in 1992 for murdering and
eating at least fifteen people in a Milwaukee killing spree
between 1978 and 1991, captured numerous small animals
as a child, tortured them and finally killed them. He loved
to parade around his home when his parents were out
with impaled frogs, cats and dogs' heads on sticks. Albert
DeSalvo, the 'Boston Strangler', killed thirteen women.
As a boy, he put cats and dogs into orange crates and shot
arrows through the slats to kill them.

There are many other examples. Ariel Castro, however,
seems to have spared God's lesser creatures during his
learning curve of cruelty, reserving his resentment for the
opposite sex. He kept dogs throughout his time as gatekeeper of his squalid empire at Seymour Avenue and even
had three – a chihuahua and two poodle-mix dogs – at the
time of his arrest. The dogs were matted and needed
grooming, but none bore the hallmarks of abuse. The
violence was kept entirely for women.

The profile of Ariel Castro is that of a classic abuser.
Feeling put upon by society, in a dead-end job with low
pay, he achieved self-regard by making others dance to his
tune. He believed it was his right to use violence and emotional abuse to control the twisted 'family' he would one

day have. He believed in the right to behave in whatever way he chose while in his own home. He had the illusion that a 'real' man should be tough, powerful and the head of the household. He believed sex was an entitlement and something to be taken from women whenever he felt like it.

He would never take responsibility for his behaviour and preferred to think loved ones, circumstances or stress provoked his violence. It was always the fault of others. He was a classic secret perpetrator in that he never used violence in other situations – around friends, bosses, work colleagues, or when police were to be seen. Only his family members witnessed the violence he dished out to his common-law wife, Grimilda.

He was, ultimately, both a coward and a bully.

Prolonged police interviews with the victims of Seymour Avenue have produced a chilling portrait of a predator whose empathy switch was turned off in childhood, probably as a means to inure himself to the emotional – and perhaps physical – pain inflicted upon him. Virtually all domestic violence experts agree that abuse is learned behaviour and that abusive people choose to abuse. Clinical studies have shown time and again how abusers' heart rates at the time they are committing their abuse are normal, and the abusers become psychologically calmer when they abuse. Abusers generally abuse, say the experts, because they've learned somewhere in the course of their lives that coercion and control work to their benefit.

In police interviews Castro later admitted to being

'addicted to sex' at an early age, unable to control his impulses and to being 'cold-blooded'. Essentially charmless with women, unable through his emotional make-up to indulge in the mating rituals that precede any normal relationship, he chose to take with violence what he couldn't get any other way.

Ricky Sanchez was another musician who played with Castro. The two men would rehearse salsa in Castro's ramshackle home amid the grime and mess of a living room where the windows were boarded up and the semi-darkness was lit by the glow of a large plasma TV screen. It was almost always on, tuned either to music, sport or programmes about sports cars.

'You always had to call ahead if you were visiting him,' said Ricky, a bass player like Castro. 'You could never go to the Seymour Avenue home unannounced. That was a complete no-no. Once a small girl appeared, and shortly afterwards I heard a thudding somewhere else in the house. Ariel said she was his granddaughter. I'd been there about forty-five minutes when she walked into the room from the corridor, from the kitchen at the back of the house. I was a regular visitor in that house and I'd never seen her before. A strange fixed grin spread across Castro's face. He asked me, "Ricky, have you met my granddaughter?" as he took her hand and led her out of the room. That's strange, I thought, I know his kids and was sure I knew all his grandkids, but I had never seen her before.

'Then, as he came back into the front room, I heard a banging noise. It was low-pitched, a thump-thump. I couldn't tell where it was coming from in that old house. Ariel just said it was his dog upstairs, and he turned the music up. I have to say the guy was a demon but he played it real cool. It was the first time that I heard any noise.

'There were just so many locks in that house. Once, after a music session, I had to ask him to help me get out! Man, what an actor that guy turned out to be. An actor with a mean streak a mile wide – although, the noise and the kid aside, there was nothing to alert me to the fact that he might be a kidnapper and a rapist.'

Ricky, like so many others, was within a hair's breadth of rumbling the whole Castro set-up. An unknown girl, an implausible identity and the strange noises. He, like so many others, did not connect the dots.

Ultimately, people like Zaida Delgado, aged fifty-eight, a family friend, saw through the facade. 'There was something not right about him. He could be flaky and off the wall. He was also arrogant, like, "I am Mr Cool, I am the best." He had an attitude, like, "I am God's gift." '

Israel Lugo, who lives three doors down from the Castro house, said his neighbour would often park the school bus outside the house between the morning and afternoon routes. 'He'd go in the house, jump on his motorcycle, take off, come back, jump in the car, take off. Every time he switched a car, he switched an outfit.'

Sometimes Castro took his 'special friend' out for a drive. That special friend was a weird mannequin police found in the house when his time was up. It was life-sized with a mop-like wig and slanted eyes. Castro liked to prop it in the back of his car and ride around town with it.

'He threatened me lots of times with it,' said Castro's nephew, 26-year-old Angel Caraballo, who says he was 'terrified' of his uncle as a little boy and unnerved by him as an adult.

'On the times I would visit, he would say, "Act up again, you'll be in that back room with the mannequin." It was flesh-coloured, had unruly hair and long eyelashes, and sometimes Castro would dress it up to make it look more realistic. He would leap out from behind closed doors with the dummy when I was just a kid. He brought me to tears with it. I hated it.'

Control also extended to the bizarre games Castro played when he took the children from his large extended family – nieces and nephews, cousins and their friends – out for lunch or sodas at fast-food restaurants. He would buy one such drink for three or four children and force them to sip it to a line he drew on the glass with a crayon. Then he would tear a single hamburger into four and order them to eat it. They were never allowed seconds.

'I was always nervous around him,' added Angel Caraballo. 'Always.'

Angel had seen the tip of the volcano, but it was barely smoking. Others were to suffer far worse than him when it finally blew.

2. Training Days

When twenty-year-old Ariel Castro met Grimilda Figueroa it was a match made in hell. A perfect match.

He hated her from the start.

Little big men like Castro, nurturing grievances against perceived slights and life's misfortunes, look for people like Grimilda to make them feel better about themselves. It was so for the power-freak Josef Fritzl in Austria, whose own wife, Rosemarie, existed at the periphery of his cruel, selfish cosmos as a vassal who was expected to do nothing but obey, concur and bow down to him. It took close to half a century, crimes of unparalleled brutality and a life sentence for Fritzl before Rosemarie was able to break free from her tormentor. Only death released poor Grimilda from the clutches of Ariel Castro.

The notice of that death was as brief as the love in her relationship was scant. Her obituary ran in the Cleveland *Plain Dealer* newspaper, the city's main printed news source, from 28 to 29 April 2012. It was short and informative but offered no clues to the horror behind Grimilda Figueroa's sad demise and the years of suffering and abuse she endured at the hands of a man whom she bore four children – a man who, she foolishly told herself so many times, loved her despite everything.

GRIMILDA FIGUEROA, 48. Loving mother, grand-mother, daughter, sister, aunt. She also leaves behind many other relatives and friends. The family will receive friends SUNDAY 6–9 P. M. AT WALTER MARTENS & SONS, 9811 DENISON AVE. (PARKING EN-TRANCE OFF W. 99 ST.), where services will be held Monday, at 10:00 A. M. Interment Riverside Cemetery.

Not much in the way of compensation for the woman who had been the personal punchbag of a tyrant. Her family were not even spared the presence of her abuser at their final farewell to her.

Grimilda – Nilda to her family – was a woman in the wrong place at the wrong time when she moved into the orbit of Castro in Cleveland, in 1980. A shy woman, awk-ward with men, imbued with low self-esteem, considering herself both unattractive and unappealing, she was the wallflower at the edges of the Latino dance halls when she was growing up. Boys avoided her like mathematics homework, and she dreamed instead of a life helping chil-dren in orphanages, believing she would never have a family of her own. This was her own distorted view, one which a predator like Castro – overweight, prematurely balding, unsuccessful with women, seeking to bolster his own grandiose, macho vision of himself – sniffed out like a shark smelling blood. He intuited that she would be a woman who would do his bidding.

Or else. Mostly, it was to be the latter.

Grimilda was raised with her five siblings in the same district in Puerto Rico as the man who would eventually be blamed for her death. She stayed in Puerto Rico until she was sixteen, when the family moved, briefly, to New York before relocating to Cleveland. She was not academically gifted and dropped out of the city's Max Hayes High School before graduating with no qualifications and few prospects.

She dreamed of meeting Mr Right, but instead had a succession of boyfriends, none of whom were interested in her beyond one or two dates. She struggled with English, but liked music, was an accomplished cook and, according to her family, a warm and compassionate individual who placed the welfare of others before her own needs. Her father, Ismail, bought a house in Cleveland's Buehrer Avenue in 1980. The house had a self-contained second floor with three bedrooms, living room, kitchen and bathroom. It was to be Grimilda's bad luck when the Castro family moved into a house across the street from her shortly afterwards, although she didn't know it then. It was her poor choice to take up with Ariel a week later. According to friends and relatives, there were no prolonged dating rituals, no flowers, wooing or declarations of undying love. This was the collision of two damaged souls – one seeking love, the other seeking control.

Grimilda's education and upbringing in the barrio provided her with none of the skills to either recognize the danger she was putting herself in or understand the means by which to change her situation. She was no reader of *Cosmopolitan*, no student of the 'how to spot abusive men' Q&As as detailed in a hundred women's magazines every week. She could not see that the mask Ariel Castro wore – as the cool salsa player, as the striving breadwinner, and

later as the level-headed school bus driver – hid a personality that was fuelled by the need to dominate, to crush.
Anyone familiar with the dynamics of an abusive relationship knows that falling prey to one has less to do with a
person's intelligence, or even their socio-economic status,
than their sheer vulnerability.

And Grimilda left a vulnerability window a mile wide
for Castro to climb through.

Dumped by a man shortly before she met him, she was
at an emotional and mental low point when he moved
into her life and began to control it. She would not know
it, and sought to get help only when it was too late, but the
man with whom she threw in her lot was possessed of all
the indicators experts say are the character hallmarks of
the serial abuser: a need to control; an overarching sense
of entitlement; selfishness and self-centredness; an air of
superiority over others; contempt for women as stupid,
unworthy, as sex object or housekeeper; possessiveness,
viewing any woman and his children by her as his property; the confusion of love with abuse, explaining away
violence as an expression of his 'deep love'; manipulative-
ness, contradictory behaviour patterns; shifting blame,
denial; and the descent into serial violence.

This was the DNA of Ariel Castro. And Grimilda, desperate for love and affection, failed to recognize him for
the beast he was.

Her younger sister Elida Caraballo, aged forty-four, lives
barely ten miles distant from the Seymour Avenue address,
in a neat house with well-kept gardens and polite neigh-

bours. Inside, on the walls, are numerous pictures of the sister she lost, but the main shrine to Grimilda lives in Elida's heart. She curses the day that Grimilda took up with Castro, but says that no one could tell from the easy-going outside manner what kind of a man lurked within the unremarkable exterior.

One week after FBI detectives returned to the Seymour Avenue lair of her sister's tormentor, in a search for more evidence, she gave an interview for this book that laid bare the injuries and pain Grimilda had suffered.

'I don't know how it happened, or what he said to her. I was just a kid, but I know he approached her, asked her to go for a drive with him and then, you know, they were like an item within two weeks. You see, Castro was this cool guy in the neighbourhood, a musician who played in bands, and Grimilda loved music. She would have been very impressed with him. I think it was only after this two weeks that they wanted to live together, and so my dad gave them the apartment upstairs. It was certainly no prolonged, slow-burn thing. It kinda happened really quickly.'

Sometimes, during the early months of their relationship, they would move for brief periods into Lillian's home. Both families knew Ariel didn't earn much in his self-employed business ventures and were keen to help the young couple out as they saved for a deposit on their first home. If there was any physical abuse in the first year of their relationship, it was kept away from the families. But it began to surface shortly after the birth of their first child, Anthony, in September 1981, when Castro was just twenty-one. Grimilda took to wearing heavy black eyeliner, and she was often shrouded in a headscarf on warm days, in a bid to hide the bruises he had inflicted upon her.

Her father, Ismail Figueroa, now seventy-five, said, 'They lived in this small apartment on the second floor of my house. I was unhappy. He regularly locked her in there. I was afraid of the guy. I know he beat my daughter, but I am an old man. I couldn't do more. He once knocked my daughter down a staircase leaving her with a broken arm and separated shoulder. Grimilda told us not to get involved. It was hard for us, but harder for her.'

'He was a monster to her,' Elida went on. She knew Castro and his hard-drinking brothers when they were growing up and never approved of her sister's relationship with him. 'I don't know why she took up with him. I never saw him exchange a kind word with her, give her a peck on the cheek, hold her hand. Nothing. He swaggered like she was his property, and I was afraid for her from the get-go. But I didn't get involved, because that was what we were taught. Besides, I was just a kid and it was none of our business, other people's relationships. Same as she would never have got involved in my personal life, later on.

'I have heard a lot about this mask that he wore, you know, all affable and friendly with his pals, but I sensed that there was something very sinister about him. He would not so much speak to her as bark orders at her. Just a couple of months into their relationship and he was really tight with her, you know? Domineering. She became his prisoner in that house. He had these old-fashioned notions that she was there to serve him, attend to his every whim, while he did nothing for her. It was always, "That's enough about you, let's talk about me!" I think we first started noticing this really controlling aspect to his character on the day Anthony was born. That's when everything really started going downhill for her. It was like the kid was only his, and he didn't want the mom to have anything to do with him.

'I went over one day, when he was out, and she came to the door looking tired and downbeat. She had on this really dowdy dress, like something your grandma must have worn, with the hem way down below the knees. "What you wearing that for, sister?" I said to her. "Because Ariel wants me to," she said. She told me he had decided that she shouldn't wear shorter skirts because guys would look at her and think she was a whore, and that he didn't want to be married to a whore. We talked some more. She said he told her she couldn't go out without his permission. He told her where to shop and what to buy – right down to the cereals for breakfast and the brand of milk in the fridge. It came to the point where he isolated her from everyone she ever knew. She never had friends any more, she saw us less and less. He even drew up a timetable saying when she could and couldn't leave the house, because of the "guys out there" who would be looking at her. Sometimes he would pretend to leave the house but wait instead downstairs. If he heard the door to their apartment opening, he would bound back up the steps to beat her.'

This was later to become a favourite tactic in Seymour Avenue. He would use it to bind the female captives to his brutal will.

'He spat at her, "I don't want no one to think that my woman is a tramp. You are mine, and you do as I say,"' Elida went on. 'I think having the child changed everything in his make-up, it made him feel more and more that she was his property and that he could control her. He locked her in the apartment. If there had been a fire, she would have been killed. There was no way out. I would have to talk to her through the door when he was out. I would say, come on, come downstairs, come out, but she would say, "No, I can't. Ariel doesn't like it." He was obsessed about control, he was always obsessive about having control. She never had a lot of confidence, and what was left of it was sure as hell beaten and bludgeoned out of her by him.

'When things got much worse, as they did, he would threaten to kill her if she ever left him. And when that time came around, there was not a lot left of her to protest. My sister would still be alive today, were it not for him. Sure, the cops came sometimes, but when they were there calming things down, he was always standing next to her, so when they said, like, "Do you want to press charges?" well, what could she say when the bastard who had done this to her was standing next to her? She just had so much fear of him, both for herself and for her kids. She was terrified, and he knew it and preyed upon it.

'I have nothing but pure hatred for him for what he did to her. And God knows what kind of damage he inflicted on his kids. The violence first started with pushing, then things escalated because the more he thought he could get away with it, the more he would try to. The pushes led to punches – to the body at first, so no one could see the bruises, but later to the head and face – and then he would end up kicking her as she cowered like a dog on the floor. I actually saw this one time when he pushed her into this big cardboard box, the kind you have from a moving company. He pushed her into it and she went down. She had done something or said something to upset him. He pushed the flaps over, like he was sealing her in, and shouted, "You stay there until I tell you to get out." She did. She was that brow-beaten by him. This was in my parents' house. I went downstairs to tell them and he chased after me, called me an interfering bitch and told me to get out of the house and stay out of their lives. But he got Grimilda out of the box when my brothers went upstairs. On more than one occa-sion they beat up on him pretty good too. They were insane with rage when they knew what he was doing to their sister. I shouldn't be pleased that they were violent to him, but I am, because he deserved nothing less. The guy is an animal. He provoked fear in my parents as well – and in his own mother. She never said anything, but I could see it in her eyes and sense it. She was afraid of him too.'

Lillian didn't know what to do any more than poor Grimilda did. She knew things were not right, because Grimilda's parents pleaded with her to intervene, to get her son to stop. In the end, as more children came, they became Grimilda's reason to stay. She was a woman with-out a profession, without a way of making money. She was old-fashioned too, and didn't think children should be brought up without a father.

Elida explained, 'She did try to leave him several times, honestly she did. But the fear of the unknown was, I

49

guess, in the end, greater than the fear of him. She feared that he might try to harm the kids as well, steal them away or perhaps even kill them as a means of hurting her. She was trapped all ways.'

Castro had a sliding scale of punishments for his partner, depending on her 'offences', according to family and friends. If she spoke without his permission, he would slap her across her face. If she cooked something he didn't like, or in a way that was not to his taste, he would punch her in the kidneys. If, God forbid, she left the house without his express permission – even if it was to go to the corner shop for milk – she would be subjected to a kicking. He frequently locked her into the apartment when he went out, often for hours at a time, leaving her parents and her sister talking to her through the door, pleading with her to allow them to get help for her. He drew up more lists of things she could and could not do, at the top of which was looking at or conversing with another man in a 'carnal way', and he controlled which TV programmes she could watch. If he returned after a long period, he would place his hand over the back of the TV to see if it had been switched on when he was out. If it had, he would check in a TV guide what programmes had been on; if he had not authorized them as being 'suitable' for Grimilda, he would beat her. The control was paramount. He was lord and master, and she was only there to obey him.

Angel Villanueva, who is married to another of Grimilda Figueroa's sisters, said he was shocked at this 'total control' that Castro exercised over his common-law wife. 'She was not allowed to go nowhere. No matter where she wanted to go, it had to be with him. Any guy who looked at her wanted to bed her, anyone she spoke with was someone she was involved with. The jealousy, the rage that was simmering inside him, you could feel it pulse off him. Nilda should have left him years before she did. She would still be alive now. Why didn't she?'

Why indeed? Satoshi Kanazawa, an evolutionary psychologist at the London School of Economics, has been fascinated by why some women stay in abusive relationships such as the one endured by Grimilda, while others find the courage to leave. In a paper on the subject he wrote:

> While most battered women eventually leave their abusers, a substantial minority (estimates range from a quarter to a third) remain in their abusive relationships. The problem is doubly puzzling from an evolutionary psychological perspective, because it emphasizes the importance of life, survival, and individual welfare. Why do so many battered women stay in their abusive relationships? What adds to the mystery is that most of the women are themselves mystified by their own choice. When pressed, however, many respond by saying, 'Because I love him'; emotional attachment to the abuser is one of the primary reasons battered women give for why they choose to stay. From an evolutionary psychological perspective, love and other emotions are proximate mechanisms that compel organisms to engage in behaviour that, in the context of the ancestral environment, would have increased their inclusive fitness. The fact that women themselves are mystified by their own

choice when they follow their emotions and stay with their violent partners seems to suggest the possible operation of evolutionary logic to which the women do not have complete conscious access. But what possible reproductive benefits can staying with violent mates have, when such women are often severely injured, sometimes killed?

From the gene-centric view of life, there is one thing more important than life itself, and that is reproductive success. Life is important, survival is important, only because you can't get laid if you are dead. Life is merely a means to reproduction. Organisms (like humans) are only vehicles for their genes, and it is the genes, not the organisms, that are in the driver's seat. If the battered woman already has children with the batterer, she may not be able to find a superior alternative mate and father for her children, because stepfathers represent probably the greatest physical danger to children. Infants and children who do not live with two biological parents face 40 to 100 times as great a chance of being injured or killed within the family as those who live with both biological parents. Thus, as terrible as living with a batterer might be for the physical welfare of the mother, the alternative – leaving him and living with another man who is not the genetic father of her children – might be even worse for the physical and reproductive welfare of her children (and thus her genes). It is therefore not entirely unreasonable to posit that women may have been selected to tolerate a certain level of non-lethal violence in their mates in order simultaneously to protect their children and to produce sexually competitive (if also wife-beating) sons.

I am emphatically NOT suggesting that women have a preference to mate with violent abusers instead of gentle, kind, and resourceful millionaires. Given the choice, any sane woman would prefer the latter to the former. Due to the highly socially structured and constrained nature of meeting people, which results in non-random mating, the choice that some women unfortunately face is often between unemployed, uneducated, unintelligent, unmotivated, alcoholic men who are violent, and unemployed, uneducated, unintelligent, unmotivated, alcoholic men who are not. My suggestion is merely that, under some circumstances, women may have been selected to prefer the former to the latter. Some (present-day) losers may be better than others, especially in the context of the ancestral environment. There is even some evidence from field experiments from four American cities that employed men are more likely to batter their wives than unemployed men.

And Ariel Castro, although often a job-hopper, was never out of work for any significant period of time. His evil slotted in perfectly with the nine-to-five routine.

Grimilda clung on to the hope that everything would be better when the couple got their own place. She nurtured the fantasy of settling down, of things changing when they had four walls to call their own, with no pressures from parents adding to the strains of an already strained relationship. She dreamed of choosing curtains from Schindler's Fabrics on Lorain Avenue and ordering reproduction Shaker furniture pieces from the Ethan Allen catalogue that was pushed through her parents' door.

But this was self-delusion of the highest order, with zero chance of coming true. Ariel Castro had no interest in spending money on furnishings and fittings: 2207 Seymour Avenue, bought in 1992, would become a testament to cheapness and cheesiness. He filled it with second-hand furniture, threadbare rugs and beds with sagging mattresses. He always found time, and money, for his cars, his beers and his guitars, but there was to be no extra cash for playing housey with Grimilda. The house was not to be the comfortable shrine to familial love that she told herself it would be. It was to morph instead into a temple of pain, and she would be the object of that pain – the perfect human guinea pig for the torments that were to come later, when she was no longer around.

What should have been a refuge was instead an extension of Castro's human mask, allowing him to carry on perfecting his cruelty with no one but Grimilda and his poor children to endure and witness it.

She should have known better. Three years before moving into the house, after having moved from the sphere of their respective families to live in a $100-a-month rented home on 98th Street, there was a particularly savage assault. It caused her to suffer a large bruise on her shoulder, and Grimilda, encouraged by her sister, plucked up the courage to report her abuser to the police. The police report shows that Castro attacked her on 30 September 1989 after his brother Onil arrived, wanting to go out drinking.

'The complainant Figueroa asked where they would go. That's when Castro became violent,' according to the police report. 'He slapped her several times in the face. When complainant Figueroa tried to run, he grabbed her and slammed her several times into a wall and several more times into a washing machine,' the report added. It also detailed how she was treated for the bruised right shoulder. She told officers that at that point she had been his common-law wife for something like nine years and that 'several times during the relationship he has assaulted me'. But she admitted that she had never filed a complaint about him before. Their eight-year-old son, Anthony, ran out of the house to get help for her at the time of the 1989 attack and was pursued by Castro. Anthony, who would go on to become a successful banker and never raise a finger against a woman, said, 'Life with my father, growing up, was abusive and painful. He was a violent, controlling man and my mother was the one who bore the brunt of his attacks, although I wasn't spared either. I left in the late 1990s and I don't think I spent another twenty minutes in it afterwards. Having that relationship with my dad all these years when we lived in a house where there was domestic violence and I was beaten as well . . . we never were really close because of that, and it was also something we never really talked about. He was a controlling and brutal ogre. Period.'

In 1993 Grimilda complained again to the police. In December of that year the police report quoted Grimilda as telling them Castro 'threw me to the ground and pummelled my body after I said something to upset him. He hit me about the head and face and kicked my body. It was one month after I had undergone surgery for brain cancer. I was afraid that he would come home in this condition [drunk] so I had already called police.'

A family member recalled this incident and told the ABC network after Castro's eventual arrest, 'He was two-faced all the time. He was nice when he was outside, but behind closed doors he was an animal. He had done terrible things to Grimilda and treated her like trash.'

Again Anthony, aged twelve at the time, was there to witness the violence. Castro chased him out of the house as he screamed and begged for him to stop. While both were out of the house she locked the door, and Castro couldn't get back in. Police arrived on the scene, he spotted them and took off on foot, running up Seymour Avenue in a bid to escape. 'He ran away when police arrived, and was chased by officers through a neighbouring yard and arrested,' the police report said.

Grimilda was invited to the police station on the following day and invited to make a statement about his abuse, but she declined. 'I don't think he meant it, not really,' she told officers.

None were surprised. Most abused women do not press charges against their tormentors.

'If they don't have the support and the knowledge to go through with what they need to do, a lot of victims stop,' said Linda D. Johanek, chief executive officer of Cleveland's Domestic Violence and Child Advocacy Center. 'Domestic violence spills over into the community all the time. At the Domestic Violence and Child Advocacy

Center, we have always known that. But now the world has seen it. It does not surprise me that Ariel Castro has a history of domestic violence. Castro's behaviour showed all the classic signs of a batterer. Domestic violence is about having power and control over another person. Classic tactics include isolation, fear, intimidation, threats, mind games, force, physical assault, rape, extremely controlling behaviour and much more. All of which Castro used.

'Some people have asked, "Why was he not convicted of domestic violence in the case of his former wife? Would this horrific abduction have happened if he were previously held accountable? Did this give Castro more confidence to continue his outlandish abusive behaviour?" Although I cannot speak to the specific case with his former wife, I can speak to the frustration of seeing domestic violence offenders not convicted, the gaps in the system, the lack of holding batterers accountable, the lack of training for professionals, lack of education and awareness and the lack of funding for programmes to assist victims. And I can speak to the fear that victims articulate every day: "I am afraid what will happen when he gets out of jail. He threatened to kill the children if I don't take him back. He said people won't believe me. I am constantly looking over my shoulder, knowing he is out there. I am trapped in my own home." Domestic violence is the number one call to the police in all major cities and in most suburbs, although most domestic violence cases do not get reported to the police.

'There is much we can do to change our systems to better understand the problem and to respond more effectively.

There are many best practices and policies that could be in place but are not. Half of the suburban police departments in Cuyahoga County are following best-practice protocols, and the other half are not. But beyond systems, many people often wonder what they can do to help. Call the police if you hear or see domestic violence, and speak to the victim about your concern. The world must stand up and speak out against violence against women. I think they would thank you in the silence of their hearts.'

Grimilda's fears, allied to her acutely low feelings of self-worth and a total lack of knowledge of the legal system, led her to retreat from a courtroom confrontation. But a city prosecutor who reviewed the file thought the attack *was* worthy of a hearing. He filed charges of domestic violence and disorderly conduct on behalf of the city, something he didn't need Grimilda's permission for. Records show that Castro pleaded guilty to disorderly conduct on 28 December and received probation. A possible prison term was avoided when a grand jury convened to hear the case declined to take the matter further because Grimilda, in her fear, refused to testify at the last moment.

The abuse continued. Elida remembers well how the hoped-for home of marital bliss remained a place of terror for all who lived in it. The bruises appeared more often and were larger, the fear and despair in her sister's eyes less well hidden. Beatings that were irregular began to become weekly, even daily, occurrences.

'I would go over to the house and be knocking at the door, and she was there and he wasn't, and I'd say, "Open the door," and she'd say, "I can't, he locked it." He broke her nose, her ribs, her arms, and he locked her in afterwards so she couldn't get out and get help. He was a bastard. Once he beat her so bad that my husband, Frank, flew into a rage.'

Frank, like everyone else who recalled Castro's ability to appear 'normal' outside the house, was astonished at the levels of violence the man was capable of. He said, 'I went for him because I just felt sorry for Nilda. I was tired of her being abused. He was so strict. On one occasion he hit her at the top of the stairs because she hadn't done something to his satisfaction and she cracked her skull. She later blamed the fall for her brain tumour.'

Elida said it was around this time that she begged her sister to leave him. 'She said she couldn't, because he would kill the kids. She was powerless, and we were powerless.'

The police maintained that they could do nothing to help if Grimilda wasn't willing to help herself.

Michael Dvorak, the prosecuting attorney for St Joseph County, Indiana, is one of many who have publicized this problem. 'Financial dependencies, pressure from the abuser and fear of retribution to themselves or their children are some of the obstacles that victims face in laying charges. Such factors frequently cause people to recant allegations, never file charges, or refrain from seeking a court order.'

Castro, of course, knew this. He could read his terrified wife like a book and was thus able to continue his Jekyll and Hyde tormenting of her – upstanding nice guy on the outside, but a demon within the four walls of his home.

However, Castro's nice-guy act also slipped from time

to time with the neighbours who generally thought so much of him.

In November 1994 Ernest Santiago, who lived next door, said Castro threatened him with a shovel when he went to check on a rental property on the other side of Castro's home on Seymour Avenue, because a piece of chain-link fence was missing. Castro 'became upset . . . and picked up a shovel and attempted to hit victim with same,' read a police report. A profile was emerging in these police filings about Castro which, if anybody had taken the time to follow up, might have given valuable clues about what sort of man he was and what sort of things he was capable of.

Sadly, Castro's crimes were still low key in a city with shootings, muggings, rapes and arson topping the crime sheets every day. It is fair to say that the authorities unwittingly aided and abetted him in his long career as a violent predator simply because they had much more important crimes to chase up and did not believe him to be anything other than the small-time bully he seemed to excel at being. They bought into the essential pettiness of the small man, in the same way as the Austrian police bought into the solid, bourgeois bona fide appearance of Josef Fritzl and, before him, Wolfgang Priklopil.

There came a chance to derail the monster-in-waiting the following year, in 1994, when a Cuyahoga County grand jury was finally impanelled to hear the 1993 abuse allegations, but Grimilda failed to testify. Later, she said that Castro saw her on the very day she was to take the stand and offered her money and a car if she didn't tell the grand jury about his beatings.

'He also told me, "You know what will happen to you if you do testify,"' Grimilda said in a statement made a decade later, when she was free of him but not free of the fear of him. 'I knew that he would find me and assault me again . . . I was unable to offer my testimony before the grand jury. I did not tell anyone about the threats.'

The case against Castro was dropped. The little big man had won again.

It is 1996. Grimilda has been Castro's common-law wife and involuntary sparring partner for sixteen years. Now with four children – Anthony, Angie, Emily and Arlene – she approached a crossroads in her life. Family, including her sister, her parents and her cousins, continued to cajole her, arguing that she would be dead unless she left him. She finally did so after another beating nearly cost her her life. Castro repeatedly kicked her in the head after she had undergone another round of therapy for her brain tumour.

'My sister told me that he was wearing these heavy working boots with steel toecaps and he got her on the floor and just kicked her and kicked her and kicked her some more,' Elida said.

Grimilda went to her mother's home and Castro, who had been spending more and more time with his mother, moved back into 2207 Seymour Avenue to claim sole possession of the house. It was at this time that he went shopping at local hardware outlets for extra-strength steel chains, deadbolts and mortise locks. The training days were over. Soon there would be others in the house who would not be able to escape so easily, who *would* pay him the respect he deserved.

Grimilda headed that autumn of 1996 to a battered women's shelter. Her children with Castro also escaped – save for Angie, who chose to stay with her father.

'If she stayed with Ariel, he would have killed her,' Grimilda's brother José says. 'She had gone to the hospital and called the police many times, but they never did anything. We'd go over to visit and he'd never let us in the house. When my parents managed to go visit her, she'd make it quick and rush them out because she was afraid he'd come back and beat on her. When she visited our house with him, she'd just stand next to him and be quiet. We knew something was wrong with him then, but we could never have imagined what would happen years down the line.'

Monica Stephens was married to Castro and Grimilda's son, Anthony. She was an outsider who came into the family and, she says, 'I instantly recognized my father-in-law for the creep he truly was. He was a guy who gave me the heebie-jeebies from the get-go. Consequently, I never had the desire to get to know him personally or very closely. During the time I was married to Anthony, both he and Grimilda shared really painful stories about how they were both beaten and locked up. He also played a lot of mind games with my ex-husband. I only visited that house once, but nothing really stood out. But nothing surprises me now when I hear about hostages in there, cos that is what his family were to him – all hostages.'

In 1996 Grimilda took up with a man called Fernando Colon. He worked as a security guard at a local hospital where she had routinely gone for treatment for her injuries sustained over the years from Castro. After two years he was her exit visa from the shelter, and she took it.

'When I saw her with the injuries, coming to the appointment at the hospital, I offered her my assistance, saying, "If I offered you some help, would you take it?" She said yes.'

Colon was – or seemed to be – the kind of man she was looking for when she first moved in with Castro. Friends and family described him as attentive, warm, caring and, unlike his new girlfriend, unafraid of the small Puerto Rican man with the gigantic temper. In short, they liked him and warmed to him in a way none of them ever did to the mean-spirited Ariel.

In 1997, Grimilda won full custody of daughters Emily and Arlene, and in 1998 she and Colon had a son. They did not marry but lived as man and wife. Colon said Castro didn't like it that Grimilda had left him. 'He was kind of upset about it, because I took the only thing he could control and abuse. He calmed down a little several years later. But between those years, we had many, many confrontations. During one of our altercations, he said, "One day I'm going to get you back, and I'm going to destroy your life."'

It seems his chance was handed to him by the Cleveland police. Although singularly unable to protect Grimilda down the years, a Cleveland detective contacted Colon in the summer of 2004 claiming he wanted to question him about sexual abuse allegations against Grimilda's daughters. Colon and Grimilda said they were aghast at the girls' sudden claims. It is understood that the Castro daughters had made a statement to police at the urging of their father.

It was as if Castro could not bear the fact that Grimilda was the one who walked out on him. His anger over Grimilda's relationship with Colon led him to take a renewed interest in his daughters, particularly the youngest, Arlene. He was a consummate manipulator and turned her against Colon.

'He would pick her up from school or from my home on Liberty Avenue,' Grimilda said in a statement made in December 2004. 'He now contacts her by telephone quite often. Mr Castro has also purchased Arlene a lot of clothing, [CDs], a Walkman and a cellphone . . . Some of the clothing is inappropriate for her age and I will not let her wear it.' Castro also promised Emily a new SUV, she said.

The damage against the man who had walked away with his property – his woman – was done. On 1 November 2004 Colon was indicted on twenty-eight counts of rape, kidnapping and molestation. 'Outside of the police station, Ariel Castro told me to go along with the complaints against Fernando Colon and he would buy me a new car,' Grimilda said in the December statement. 'I told him that I don't need anything from him. Castro was laughing and excited. He told me that he [Colon] would know what it's like to be on the other side of the badge. Castro then suggested that we all go out to dinner. Castro believes that we will be together again.'

As the prosecution against Colon progressed, the Castro daughters moved away from Cleveland, away from their father's influence and a house where he already had other – captive, unwilling – tenants. This, Colon said, merely allowed Castro to resume his threatening behaviour towards Grimilda, even though the case had not yet gone to trial.

In August 2005 Grimilda requested a temporary restraining order against Castro, saying he had threatened to kill her and her daughters three or four times during the course of the year. The thirty-six-page document is still available to peruse on the internet and speaks of repeated threats to harm Grimilda and steal her children from her.

'She twice suffered a broken nose, had both her shoulders dislocated and her ribs injured, in addition to a knocked-out tooth. He threatened to kill [Ms Figueroa] and daughters 3 / 4 times just this year,' the paperwork said, specifying that he 'most recently threatened to kill her on 8/25/05 and the children also.'

Documents contained in the court filing disclose that Grimilda Figueroa was, in January 1997, awarded full custody of the couple's children: Anthony, Angie, Emily and Arlene. 'Nevertheless, [Mr Castro] frequently abducts [his] daughters and keeps them from [their] mother,' the domestic violence file against him said.

Grimilda asked the court in 2005 to pass a protection order banning her husband from contacting her or their children, and from harassing, stalking or bothering them. She requested that he be made to attend counselling for substance abuse and violence, and specified that the order should 'keep [him] from threatening to kill [her]'. A temporary protection order valid for a year was granted on 29 August 2005. It instructed Mr Castro to stay away from his family and banned him from owning a deadly weapon, taking drugs or drinking alcohol.

Shortly before Colon's trial, Grimilda said her daughters were getting cold feet about testifying. Private investigator Chris Giannini, who was employed by Colon to help his defence in the case, said Grimilda had called him on 25 August 2005 to say that Castro threatened to kill her if the girls did not testify: this led to her seeking the protection order against Castro a few days later. In the police report she claimed that Castro had threatened to 'beat your ass' in front of their daughters. A spokeswoman for Cleveland Mayor Frank Jackson said that police told her to go to the county prosecutor's office and file a criminal complaint, but she did not. Instead, she sought a civil order of protection in the county court.

'In Ohio, a victim can get a civil order without criminal charges because they believe this will be less upsetting to the offender,' said Anne Murray, director of the domestic violence and stalking unit for the city of Columbus, 140 miles from Cleveland.

The case was later dropped because Figueroa's attorney did not appear for a hearing. Figueroa had fourteen days to object to the temporary protection order being rescinded. She did not.

'That breaks my heart,' Murray said.

The trial against Colon went ahead. Colon's case was heard without a jury, and he was represented by an attorney who is no longer a member of the bar. Giannini gave evidence that he thought Castro, whom he had interviewed before the trial, was untrustworthy, as was the girls' testimony.

'Both daughters testified very vaguely. "Yeah, Fernando touched me." It was very vague; it was so vague it was unbelievable,' Giannini said.

Castro testified against Colon. But his son, Anthony, and Grimilda both spoke up for Colon. Colon's court-appointed attorney was Robert A. Ferreri, who had been admitted to Ohio's state bar in 1980 but suspended twice, in 1999 and 2000, according to documents on the Ohio Supreme Court's website. In 2011, Ferreri resigned from the law as he faced further disciplinary matters. According to court documents, his resignation is 'unconditional, final and irrevocable'.

During the hearings, Ariel Castro took to the stand to deny that he had ever abused his common-law wife. Instead, he said, Grimilda had tried to get physical with him, once hitting her head on a door jamb in the process, which resulted in a trip to the hospital. He also denied threatening Colon and Figueroa, and said he had gone to the police immediately after hearing Arlene and her friend talking about Colon's alleged inappropriate sexual behaviour. When asked if anyone lived with him at his house on Seymour Avenue – the address where police recovered Berry, DeJesus and Knight – he said, 'No.'

Which, by then, was another lie. Castro, the master manipulator, had three women in his grip and the world didn't suspect a thing.

The indictment of Colon originally contained twenty-eight counts, including rape and kidnapping. The judge acquitted Colon of most of the charges, but convicted him of four counts of gross sexual imposition. Colon was sentenced to three years' probation and is now a registered sex offender in Ohio.

Grimilda was astonished that the girls had testified against him. 'I am a stay-at-home mom,' she said in a statement made in December 2004. 'I have never seen any inappropriate conduct between Fernando Colon and any of my children. If anything inappropriate had occurred, my daughters would have been quick to tell me.'

It didn't help. Colon is now a free man, but in name only.

On the day of sentencing, Colon said, he learned that Grimilda was relocating to Fort Wayne, Indiana, where her children now lived. The pair broke up soon afterwards. Colon is unemployed and unemployable. No one, he says, wants to offer employment to a convicted child molester. He maintains that he was the victim of Castro.

Elida, the sister who knew more about Grimilda's suffering than anyone else, believes him. 'Of course he was set up. Castro did this to him. He fooled the authorities into charging an innocent man. It was Castro's revenge, pure and simple.'

'I absolutely thought that I was going to win,' Colon said. 'It was heartbreaking for me, because I knew my life practically was over. So I was really upset and hurt at the same time.' When news of Castro's arrest broke, Colon's mother called him from Puerto Rico, sobbing. 'She said, "I told you that all you had to do is have faith and something would come out." I didn't do this thing and I am convinced that he was behind my woes. That's what he

68

does – he manipulates and he lies and he hurts. He won in the end. I went to jail, and I lost Grimilda, and she lost her life.

'He's like a human cyclone, destroying everything in his wicked path. He is a monster, the exact opposite of what so many people thought him to be. I am glad he is in jail now and that the world knows him for what he is. Glad because he deserves to suffer, but more importantly because he fitted me up for a fall and I now have a chance to clear my name.

'Nine years ago I told two FBI agents to investigate Castro in connection with the disappearances of Amanda Berry and Gina DeJesus, because I had this gut feeling about the guy. But they weren't interested in my tip. They came to quiz me after the disappearance of Gina DeJesus in 2004. Because I was, by then, the stepfather of Arlene, Castro's daughter with Nilda, and Gina DeJesus was Arlene's best friend. It was natural that they would come calling.

'I was also the last adult person to see Gina before she vanished. Arlene Castro and Gina walked to Westown Square, the nearby shopping centre where I worked as a security officer. Arlene asked me if Gina could come over and spend the night. When I said no, the girls tried to get around me "by checking with mom" via a public pay-phone. The girls got a second no from her. I saw them walk away. But before they did, there was another phone call – this one to Ariel Castro. The girls split up and Castro came back and picked her up. That's what I figured, and that's what I told the Feds. They gave me a polygraph as they quizzed me about Gina – I guess to make sure I wasn't a suspect – and I passed it. But they never followed up on my suspicions.

'In addition to Arlene's close friendship with DeJesus, Castro's older daughter, Emily, was friends with Amanda Berry, who had disappeared nearly a year earlier. I said that if you're talking to me because of my stepdaughters, you should really be talking to Ariel Castro. He has more chance and opportunity than I do. These girls are best friends with his daughters. The agents told me, "Well, we have to deal with you. Whatever arises in the case, we'll take care of that." I do not know if they ever followed up and questioned Castro, but from what I read in recent weeks, I guess not.'

The FBI later said that it had 'scrubbed' its records on the case, but believed that Colon had made no mention of his suspicions about Ariel Castro when he was questioned.

Colon added, 'Castro peppered my house with abusive phone calls and threatened me. He told me very clearly, "One day I'm going to get back at you and I'm going to ruin your life." He waited for that moment and then accused me of something that does the most damage to a person. Castro made the molestation accusations in July 2004, two months after DeJesus vanished. I think he did it to get police attention away from him. By that point he had all three kidnapped women under his roof.'

In the paperwork of the local Ohio civil court dealing with family matters can be found the last written testimony of Grimilda against the man she unwisely chose as a partner. In it she detailed how, in several attacks, Castro twice broke her nose, broke three ribs, knocked out a tooth, left her with a blood clot on the brain and dislocated both of her shoulders when he hoisted her up on a chain he had fitted to an iron hook installed in the concrete ceiling of the basement at Seymour Avenue. Her attorney, Robert Ferreri, requested that a judge 'keep Castro from threatening to kill my client'.

Grimilda's life was brutal, nasty and filled with pain, ending on 25 April 2012, just a little over a year before the world would learn how brutal and nasty the father of her children really was. She died of the painkillers prescribed for the brain tumour which had plagued her for years.

The painkiller oxycodone ended her days, but her family are in no doubt whatsoever about what really took her life: Ariel Castro killed her.

'I actually saw him at her funeral and, man, we wanted to do something to him,' José Figueroa, her brother, recalls. 'My father had to pull me back and remind me that it was a funeral and it was no place for fighting. But we all didn't like him for what he did to Grimilda. Everyone knew he was up to something. Ariel mistreated my sister for years. I believe he murdered my sister. He abused her for years. She had multiple instances of serious head trauma and it created a brain tumour in her head.'

Her sister Elida added, 'There was so much severe pain. And Castro and a brother turned up uninvited to her wake, drank heavily and cracked jokes. She couldn't even stand up towards the end. If she did, she would fall straight to the ground. She was partially paralysed. It's not just us say he killed her – she blamed it all on Ariel too. Everybody needs to know that my sister was abused by him. She was a victim. She didn't do anything but cook, clean and take care of her kids, and this is how he repaid her.'

Elida regrets that her daughter Elida-Marie, now nineteen, visited Castro's house in Seymour Avenue two years before his dark secret was exposed. Elida's husband, Frank, said, 'She told us that the only thing he said was, "You stay in this room, and do not go in any other room. I want you to stay in this room only." She took it as him being rude. But she said he would always turn the radio up high. And before anybody could even visit, you'd have to wait thirty-five or forty minutes before he would let you in. It was creepy. He was creepy.'

The family are bitter that Grimilda's death was for nothing. Had police or other agencies acted more strongly against Castro, then he might have been on the radar and could have been thwarted at the start of his diabolical plans for Seymour Avenue, rather than after ten years. A trawl of all police files, for this book, show that Cleveland police were summoned six times to handle accusations that Castro had assaulted or menaced people, including the three beatings of his wife. Other incidents included a complaint that Castro had threatened to run over a man while dropping his children off at a bus stop in 1996, and another neighbour made a complaint to the police in the same year, telling officers that Castro threatened, 'I'm going to get you, bitch!' as he drove past her house. The dispute was apparently over a fence.

It is unclear whether any of the incidents could have led police to the three women Castro had kidnapped as sex slaves. But the number of times his name pops up in the Cleveland police database is far more than the two incidents police originally reported when his crimes were discovered in 2013.

One in every four American women will experience domestic violence in her lifetime, according to the National Coalition Against Domestic Violence. An estimated 1.3 million women are victims of physical assault by an intimate partner each year, but most cases of domestic violence are never reported to the police. Americans, say experts, are conditioned to view domestic 'disputes' as private matters. Many think it isn't their place to judge a stranger's personal life and even stray into the morally dubious realm of, 'Who knows? Maybe she deserved it.'

Disturbing evidence of this mindset, the mindset which undoubtedly contributed to Grimilda's sufferings, is exemplified by an ex-girlfriend mannequin on sale at the 2013 National Rifle Association convention in Houston, Texas. The company, Zombie Industries, advertised the mannequin, called Alexa, like this:

Be warned, hell hath no fury like a woman scorned but a man scorned is nothing to mess with. A young gent from Louisiana – we'll call him Andre, to protect his identity – was deeply committed to his one true love and her to him, or so he thought. While partying with her friends during one particular Mardi Gras, she took several suitors over the course of the festivities.

As feminist writer Katie Baker commented, 'In other words, the bitch was asking for it.' She added, 'We should also care about men who abuse their wives and children before they go out and find replacements to hide in the basement.' She said that calls which neighbours of Castro claimed were made about strange goings-on at the house – one involving an alleged sighting of a captive being walked like a dog on a lead – could be significant. 'If the cops are lying about ignoring Castro's neighbours' calls, that implies they were unconcerned about a man who had a record of being abnormally and dangerously cruel to women and children. If the neighbours are lying about making those calls in the first place, that probably means they suspected something was up underneath Castro's jovial mask and wish they had spoken up sooner. Both conclusions show that we're not adequately enraged by domestic violence unless it seems ripped from the head-lines of *Law & Order*.'

Clearly, there may have been opportunities down the years for the police to have become involved. Sexual, physical, mental abuse – all these things were happening under his roof. But the daughters said nothing, and Grimilda said little. Like most domestic violence, it stayed behind four walls and locked doors.

'He is dead to me,' said Angie Griggs, the daughter who grew up in the vortex of violence at Seymour Avenue, of her father. 'He is the most evil, vile, demonic criminal I can imagine. Of course, I only knew him as a daddy's little girl. To me he was a friendly, caring, doting man and the violence against Mom was only seen by me occasionally, although I understand things better now as an adult. Now he can never be Daddy again. I have no sympathy for the man, both for how he treated Mom and how he treated those girls. I am just sad to think that I didn't know anything extraordinary was going on in that house when I was growing up.

'When Mom and Dad were fighting, it's like I just wanted to melt into the ground. I've seen him basically stomp on her like she was a man. It was weird when they split. I stayed with him. I kinda foolishly believed the excuses he made for the violence, although of course there are no excuses at all, least not valid ones. I finished my growing up under his roof. Now I am so ashamed of him. I just hope people realize it was him and only him and that we, the rest of us who carry his name, do not carry the blood of a monster in our veins. I miss Mom and I wish I could have done more, but others should have done more too.'

At Grimilda's funeral her family played the famous Céline Dion song 'My Heart Will Go On', a ballad of romantic love that was her favourite. A romantic love that she was never to find. The epitaph her son, Anthony, posted on the funeral home online guest book was the most poignant:

Dear Mom. You are gone too soon. But your suffering is over.

He goes every month to the Riverside Cemetery in Cleveland to leave fresh flowers upon her grave.

3. Missing, Believed Dead

He had waited, he had plotted, he had dreamed. He had seen off that bitch of a wife, Nilda, and he had become bored with porn. The house was ready. He was ready.

It was show time.

Ariel Castro was the little man with the big plan. His sense of hatred towards women was palpable, had been ever since he had a sex drive of his own. But the mask stayed in place, the disguise of affability and normality rarely slipped in the 'hood. He would use it to effect this day, 22 August 2002. But no more Mr Nice Guy – at least, not for that little whore Michelle. Now she would really know who was boss.

Castro waited in his car in the cloying heat of the midsummer day, the air conditioning switched off. He liked it hot. He was parked on Lorain Avenue, the artery through the barrio that was to be his hunting ground. As he waited, he turned up the car radio and tapped his fingers on the steering wheel to the Latino rhythm that blasted from the speakers. There she was, walking along, as if nothing had happened.

'It's your unlucky day, bitch,' he said to himself as he turned the key in the ignition of his Toyota and the engine fired up. Pulling alongside, smoothly, he wound down the window. He offered her a ride home. She had no money. She had no training not to accept lifts from strangers – but then again, Ariel wasn't exactly a stranger. Not exactly.

'I just got to spin by my house to collect something, sugar, on the way. That's not a problem, is it?'

The diminutive woman, aged just twenty-one, nodded that it wasn't. She told him about Joey, about her pain.

Castro devised an instant plan. He told her he had a cute puppy dog at his house and that he was looking for a good home for it. He told her she could have it as a gift for her son when they got back together. Michelle brightened instantly. And when Ariel had rolled his car up to the driveway of 2207 Seymour, it was no problem at all for her to step inside, just for a minute, to have a coffee while he collected the dog and whatever else he had stopped for. The dying rays of the sun shone on her as she manoeuvred around the junk collection at the bottom of his concrete yard and through the back door into his home.

There was no puppy for her.

Goodbye Michelle.

Michelle Knight, the first of Castro's captives and the one who endured the worst treatment, was a victim long before that fateful day when she first fell into his clutches. Michelle, like Natascha Kampusch (who vanished off a Vienna street at the age of ten), was an unhappy child with a tortured family life. And, like Natascha, she soon slipped off the radar of the authorities. Both were victims of a kind of inborn prejudice – perhaps subconscious – against poor people. People whose lot in life seemed to mark them down as losers. People who, critics would allege, warranted less attention from the authorities than others. The candles would be burned and the vigils held for the young women who would follow Michelle into the hell that was Castro's home, but Michelle became simply a distant memory in the minds of most. And sometimes barely a paragraph, if that, in the stories that chronicled the fate of her compatriots.

Life for Michelle was rough from the start. She was, in the common parlance of her teachers and family, a 'slow' child, perhaps displaying Asperger's symptoms, although the syndrome was never diagnosed. Michelle's mother, Barbara Knight, now living in Naples, Florida, says her daughter spent most of her life growing up on Cleveland's west side, helping her work in the vegetable garden, listening to bedtime stories that were read to her, dreaming of owning a puppy. Sister to a twin boy, Freddie, she was enthralled by fire engines as a child and decided to become a firefighter later in life, until the day she helped her mother deliver a neighbour's pet of a litter of puppies and set her heart on becoming a vet instead.

Since her daughter's return from the house of horrors, Mrs Knight has tried to paint a picture of normality for Michelle, of an upbringing that was like most other children's – with good times and bad times, but essentially correct and decent. Hers was a rose-tinted view of childhood which included feeding apples to the neighbour's pet pony, eating ice cream together at the lakeside every Sunday, cuddling up on the family sofa to watch favourite TV programmes and enjoying family meals. It is a wholesome, friendly picture.

It just doesn't happen to be true.

Social workers were involved with the Knight family

from the earliest days. There was friction with Michelle's mother, with her neighbours, with teachers at school and fellow pupils. Her medical condition often led to her being confused about her surroundings and landed her with a cruel nickname at junior high school: Dopey (as in the intellectually challenged Disney dwarf). Her own father was long gone from the family home on West 60th Street. Then, at the age of just seventeen, a terrible fate befell her. Long bullied at school for being different, the baiting took an entirely different turn when three predatory boys at the school cornered her in a deserted storeroom and gang-raped her.

'They just grabbed her by the arm and, one by one, took her, just like that,' said her great-aunt Deborah Knight. 'Weren't nothing she could do about it.'

She was left bruised, bleeding, dazed – and pregnant. The end result of this attack, besides the obvious trauma, was a son she called Joey and to whom she was devoted. She dropped out of high school, all plans for a career working with animals now abandoned. She also experienced what she viewed as justice for 'poor people'. She told the police about what happened to her, but rape charges against the boys were never filed. 'The police just didn't seem to take it seriously,' her mother said later. The same charge would be levelled against them when it came to looking for her during the long years of her singular martyrdom.

After Joey was born, she continued to live with her mother, Barbara, and twin brother, Freddie. With her father gone, her mother took up with a man called David

Feckley. Feckley was an erratic, self-obsessed violent con-
troller of the type that would later abduct Michelle.

Police records show that in the early 2000s he was convicted of child endangerment, after breaking Michelle's
infant son's arm. One indictment filed listed thirty-five
criminal counts, including charges of 'endangering children, rape with notice of prior conviction and repeat
violent offender specifications, gross sexual imposition,
intimidation, and felonious assault with notice of prior
conviction and repeat violent offender specifications'. He
pleaded guilty to endangering children and felonious
assault with notice of prior conviction and repeat violent
offender specifications. A sentencing hearing was held on
26 August 2002. At the hearing, Detective Daniel Ross testified about the injuries sustained by the victim, as well as
the medical report, statements made by the victim's mother
and grandmother concerning threatened violence by Feckley, a history of domestic violence in the household,
including prior abuse of the child, and Feckley's lack of
remorse.

Following the detective's testimony, the trial court
reviewed Feckley's prior record and read portions of the
pre-sentence investigation report. The trial court then
sentenced Feckley to the maximum eight-year sentence
for endangering children and the maximum eight-year
sentence for felonious assault, to run concurrently.

Michelle also alleged that her stepfather raped her. This
would have gone to court too – except for the fact that
she couldn't be found for the hearing, scheduled to take
place on 26 August 2002. This was because, by the time

the legal system got around to dealing with the case, she was living somewhere else. At 2207 Seymour Avenue, the unwilling lodger of another monster, another rapist.

And this tenancy looked set to be for life.

Michelle had been visiting her cousin, at her home at West 106th Street and Lorain, the day she was taken. She was at the lowest possible ebb in her life. Almost friendless, with few prospects and a domestic life in shreds, she had also lost her most precious possession – her son, Joey. Social services had taken the child away from her a few weeks before she was taken by Castro, worried that her increasingly erratic behaviour was an indication that she was not, and never could be, a fit mother. On the day that her life changed for the worse, she was due to attend a custody hearing into her son's future. It was an appointment she never made. Joey is now a teenaged boy, with a different identity, believed to have been adopted by another family. It remains unclear at the time of writing whether Michelle will ever see him again.

Her mother, Barbara, implores her for a reunion, saying, 'Certain people said she didn't want nothing to do with me. But still, in my heart, I thought no, because I knew my Michelle. They figured she just left because of the baby and everything.'

But Michelle, in all the long years of captivity in the house of her abductor, often saw and heard radio and TV news reports charting the searches and the hope of a community of finding her and her compatriots in misery. She heard little about her own family organizing such things, and that pain left scars as deep as any inflicted upon her by Castro. Her disappearance rang the usual alarm bells among family and friends, but they all believed there was an underlying cause: she had flipped out over the continuing legal battle to regain custody of Joey and had simply run away.

An unanswered question in the case is: did her abductor know her, or at least know of her? I believe the answer is almost certainly yes. Daughters of Ariel Castro knew the other two victims he abducted, providing their father with fresh prey through their own innocent friendships with them. But there seemed no tangible connection between Michelle and him. Except, of course, that he was a man who knew the area better than most. He was a school bus driver, so he drove around the locality every day. He was out on Lorain Avenue most evenings, heading to a fast-food joint for his takeaway dinners. He had that indefinable instinct of the predator looking to take someone weaker, someone damaged, someone unable to fight back. Like Wolfgang Priklopil taking Natascha Kampusch in broad daylight when she was not even eleven years old.

Castro had watched, unseen, and had got away with it. In his car, from his bus, on his motorcycles, he would have seen Michelle, looking like a little girl lost on the broad sidewalks, perhaps sometimes even with Joey. Everything Castro did was acted out according to some kind of inner timetable, a master plan. It is inconceivable that Michelle was not 'chosen' like the others, because that is simply the way Castro worked. Random was not an option he was comfortable with.

And so it was with Michelle. Wrong place, wrong time,

wrong guy. For Castro, for his needs, she was the perfect, damaged, subservient woman-child of his dreams.

Terrible things awaited Michelle when Castro tricked her into his home. It wasn't until Amanda Marie Berry went missing on 21 April 2003, one day before her seventeenth birthday, that Michelle had a fellow prisoner with whom to share her suffering – one who, in the twisted rationale of the captor, was to be a princess to Michelle's Cinderella character.

Sadly, Cinderella was also the role assigned to Michelle by both her family and the police. When she went missing, the immediate assumption by all was that she had simply run away, shattered at the decision by social services to take Joey, the one good thing in her otherwise wretched life, away from her. Because she was an adult, perhaps because she was troubled, Michelle's disappearance was never to become the stuff of town meetings and candlelit vigils.

Her family were later to blame the police for 'not taking it seriously' when she went missing, but thousands of adults go missing in America every year, many of them simply to start new lives in new states. She was soon a name and a number in a ledger – and barely fifteen months later, even that was erased.

Tiffani White, a relative, said, 'No one was looking for Michelle Knight.'

Only when she was found did Michelle Knight's mother claim that she had never felt the police conclusion was 'convincing'. She said she had never believed her daughter would simply vanish without so much as a phone call.

Deputy Police Chief Ed Tomba was forced to admit,

after the girls were rescued, that while his department had 'poured resources' into the search for Amanda and Gina, Michelle was 'the focus of very few tips'.

The initial missing persons report noted that Michelle had a 'mental condition' that made her easily confused by her surroundings. A cousin, Brenda Dinickle, said that Michelle had 'the mind of a child. I thought she ended up dead.'

She might well have been. The FBI pulled her from the nationwide missing persons database the following year, claiming that repeated attempts to contact her mother, with whom Michelle had enjoyed a strained relationship at the best of times, had failed.

The official policy on investigating missing adults at the time stated that an officer must go and see if a missing person has been found, then inform the FBI within two hours so the person can be removed from the National Crime Information Center database. Kym Pasqualini, a national advocate for missing adults, said that the removal of Michelle's name and description from the database 'helped the case fall through the cracks'. But despite this bureaucratic foul-up, officers did continue to make inquiries about her whereabouts afterwards, successfully verifying in May 2003 that she was still unaccounted for after finally contacting her mother. Mrs Knight said she would often put up fliers around Cleveland's west side, even after moving away, and claimed she would often return to continue the search on her own as police were 'little help'.

The simple fact is, the disappearances of Amanda and Gina made big news in Cleveland and Michelle's did not.

Justin Peters, a crime reporter for the *Slate* news

website, said, 'Why didn't the Cleveland cops pay more attention to Knight's disappearance?'

Perhaps because ignoring adult missing persons reports seems to have been de facto departmental policy for many years. The lax investigation into Knight's disappearance doesn't appear to have been an isolated incident. In 2009, Cleveland resident Anthony Sowell was arrested and charged with kidnapping, raping and murdering eleven women between 2007 and 2009. (Sowell disposed of the bodies in and around his east side home, blaming the ensuing stench on his ageing stepmother and also on a nearby sausage shop.) Afterwards, victims' relatives claimed that the Cleveland Police Department was slow to investigate or connect the disappearances, which allowed Sowell to continue his predatory actions. Sometimes, the police counselled family members not to bother filing missing persons reports at all, saying that 'there is no use in filing a report if the missing person is an adult'.

Mayor Frank Jackson addressed the criticisms by appointing a panel to review police procedures in missing persons cases. The ensuing report issued twenty-six recommendations regarding how the department could improve, such as creating a dedicated missing persons unit, developing a missing persons website and training officers on how to handle these types of investigations. As of April 2012, twenty-two of the recommendations had been implemented. As the *Slate* news website noted:

If these policies had been in place when Michelle Knight went missing, would they have helped the police solve the case or rescue the missing women any sooner? Maybe, maybe not. At the very least, a more conscientious investigation into Knight's disappearance might have led the police to connect it with the subsequent disappearances of Amanda Berry and Gina DeJesus from the exact same neighbourhood. The fact that Knight seems to have been quickly dismissed as just another troubled woman who ran away from home counts as a definite demerit against the Cleveland PD.

The state's website for missing people says:

The Ohio Attorney General's Office through the Bureau of Criminal Investigation Missing Persons Unit assists local law enforcement and families in locating and recovering missing children and adults. The unit issues Endangered Missing Child Alerts, Endangered Missing Adult Alerts, and is involved in issuing Amber Alerts and Blue Alerts in coordination with local law enforcement. Staff members aid in searches for missing children and adults using social media, public records, law enforcement databases, and other resources.

Amber alerts are for children who are thought to have been kidnapped. Immediate notification is sent to all law enforcement bodies in the area where the child vanished, together with urgent appeals being made to the media to publicize the case. Law enforcement agencies and broadcasters use the Emergency Alert System (EAS), formerly called the Emergency Broadcast System, to air a description of the missing child and suspected abductor. (The same concept is used during severe weather emergencies.) 'The goal of the Amber Alert is to promptly involve entire communities to assist in the search for and safe return of abducted children,' says Ohio State's official policy. The Blue Alerts are to find the suspected wounders or killers of police officers.

Michelle fell through the cracks; she was too old to be a child, and she was not a police officer. Consequently, she warranted no colours at all. She had left her cousin's house and was barely four miles from home when she took the ride she should never have accepted.

Incredible though it may seem, Castro had a girlfriend for much of the time he held Michelle in captivity. Her name is Lillian Roldan – from Puerto Rico, like him – and while she has never spoken publicly about their affair, she later described their relationship to prosecutors as 'normal'. According to Ms Roldan, Castro broke off the relationship because he had 'too many other commitments'.

This was shortly before he planned the next addition to his secret family.

Castro congratulated himself that things had gone well with the bitch Michelle during the months he had held her captive. There had been no foolish attempts at escape, no nosy neighbours prying. He had bent her to his will. Now it was time to expand the franchise – what he called, in his twisted mind, the 'sex on a shelf' products.

Amanda Berry was last heard from when she called her sister to tell her that she was getting a ride home from her job at a Burger King outlet at West 110th Street and Lorain Avenue. The call came around 7.45 p.m. on 21 April 2003. 'I've got a ride. I'll call you back.' Just three blocks, a picket fence, a row of tulips, a few hedges and a chain-link fence separated her from the safety of her home on West 111th Street, a home where she had stashed $100 to buy herself a new dress for her seventeenth birthday the next day.

Again, the predator was waiting, the car idling by the kerbside, the salsa music playing from the radio. He had just dropped his daughter Angie off at his mother's house and had seen Amanda walking along a few minutes earlier. Angie had waved at her and she had waved back. So when he pulled up alongside her, she believed that Angie was still in the vehicle. He asked her if she remembered his son, Anthony, who used to work at Burger King, and she did. He offered her a ride home. He didn't seem like a stranger, so she agreed. En route, he said that his daughter was at home. Did Amanda want to see her there? She said OK.

His daughter Angie said, after her father's sordid world had been revealed in May 2013, that it sickened her that he had used her as a means to lure victims. But that is what monsters do.

'Mandy' Berry was living just a few miles away from Seymour Avenue in 2003. She had attended Wilbur Wright Middle School with Castro's daughter Emily – a friend, at that time, but someone who is now serving a lengthy jail sentence for attempting to kill her own baby by slashing its throat. The psychological problems of Ariel Castro did not, it seems, end solely with him. Mandy, too, was a child

1. The house at 2207 Seymour Avenue in Cleveland, Ohio, where Ariel Castro kept Michelle Knight, Amanda Berry and Gina DeJesus locked up for over a decade.

2. Tito DeJesus Jr., a friend and bandmate of Ariel Castro, with a picture of Castro on his phone. The picture was taken around a decade ago.

3. The grocery store run by Ariel Castro's uncle, Cesi, opposite Seymour Avenue.

4. Belinda's nightclub, where Castro played the bass guitar.

5. Grimilda Figueroa, the common-law wife of Ariel Castro who died of a brain tumour in 2012.

6. Elida Caraballo, Grimilda Figueroa's sister. The family believe that Grimilda died from the horrific injuries inflicted on her by Castro during the sustained beatings.

7. Michelle Knight. Castro's first kidnap victim, the then 21-year-old Michelle was abducted in 2002.

8. Model of the inside of 2207 Seymour Avenue, displayed in the courtroom during Castro's trial.

9. A heavy curtain covered the steps leading down to the cellar, where Castro would chain the women to the 'punishment pole' and beat them repeatedly.

10. The cellar. To the left is the 'punishment pole', which ran from the ceiling to the floor and was held in place by steel bolts.

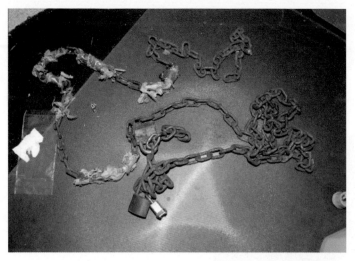

11. Metal chains which Castro would fasten to the basement pole and bedroom walls to ensure that the women couldn't escape.

12. The motorcycle helmet Castro made the women wear to muffle their screams while he raped them.

13. Amanda Berry, Castro's second victim. She was taken in 2003, the day before her seventeenth birthday, on her way home from her job at the local Burger King.

14. The Burger King on the junction of West 110th Street and Lorain where Amanda Berry was taken by Castro.

15. Gina DeJesus, who was kidnapped in 2004 when she was just fourteen years old.

16. The corner at West 105th Street and Lorain, where Gina went missing. Castro was out on Lorain Avenue most evenings, heading to a fast-food joint for his takeaway dinners.

17. The payphone where Gina DeJesus was last seen making a call as she was returning home from school.

with some of the problems of Michelle Knight and the Castro offspring.

Victoria Kempton, a friend of her mother's, claimed that her father, Johnny, was constantly in and out of jail as a juvenile and handy with his fists when he took up with her mother. 'Louwana, Amanda's mom, would come over to our house with bruises after getting beatings from him,' she said. 'After Amanda was born he was put away again, and she used to come over to use our phone to call him in jail. Louwana left him, taking Amanda with her when she was about four.'

Amanda was raised by her mother, who had named her after a Conway Twitty song, 'Amanda Light Of My Life'. She seemed to have shrugged off the earliest memories of a turbulent childhood and became an ordinary, happy girl who liked to put posters of her favourite pop stars on the wall of her bedroom – Eminem being one of them – and dreamed in her teen years of becoming a fashion designer. She devoured glossy magazines detailing the latest dresses and styles, which she copied into notebooks she kept by her bedside.

Tina Miller, Amanda's cousin, told American celebrity magazine *People*, 'She was hyper-organized, loved Eminem, loved the movie *8 Mile*. She was close to her nieces. She had just bought a cellphone before she went missing. She was always so smart. Mandy was always in the magnet programmes in school. I recall going to her house, and whatever song was playing, Mandy knew.' Tina said her cousin also had a passion for pop music and for clothes, particularly the designer brands Tommy Hilfiger and Nautica. 'But she refused to cross-contaminate,' she added. 'It was either all Tommy or all Nautica.' She may have been a 'girly girl', but she was also 'a little firecracker. I remember Mandy having a smart mouth.'

Every summer Amanda and her family travelled south to Elizabethton in Tennessee to visit relations. She loved the countryside, the rivers, the wildlife and the soft velvet-coloured sky at night. Her father lived there with his parents. 'She had the nickname Commando Amando. That's what I nicknamed her when she was little. She loved to fight with me, and she was such a good kid. A tomboy, wasn't no pushover girl,' said John Berry. That toughness, he believes, was what pulled her through what was to befall her.

Amanda loved her low-paid job at Burger King, putting aside a little money each week to give to her mother, saving a little more for the course she hoped to take in fashion design when she was eighteen. She was doing well at online school, was liked by her friends and her co-workers at Burger King, and was on course to graduate early. She nurtured dreams of working for the great Parisian couture houses when she grew up – Chanel or Dior.

One of her pals, Darrell Ford, was working with her on the night she vanished. He said, 'Amanda was a great person, fun to be with, concerned for others, caring, just really nice. When she went, I was stunned – and I was even more stunned when she resurfaced. I mean, what did he do to her for ten years? It doesn't bear thinking about.'

Amanda, who is five feet one inch tall, and weighs 110 pounds, had dated boys since her high school years, but none seriously. She had a pierced left eyebrow and a hernia scar across her stomach from when she was a child (which she hid with blouses or long shirts). Friends said she cared about her appearance but was not a fanatic about looks. She liked having her nails done, though, and had an appointment on the day of her birthday for a manicure. She smoked Newport cigarettes, which she kept in a black shoulder bag along with her slim, silver-coloured mobile phone.

'The last time I saw her,' her mother said, just days after she disappeared, 'it was "I love you, have a good day at work."'

That night, the night she never came back, her three- and four-year-old nieces were disappointed because she was due to curl up on the sofa with them and watch TV.

The alarm bells rang with the Cleveland police, and Amanda Berry became a missing person of some note. But no one connected the fact that Michelle Knight had gone missing in the same area, as she was judged to be a runaway. The spotlight never fell on the nice guy of Seymour Avenue who offered her a ride home.

But first, she was just going to step into his house to see his daughter.

Amanda felt a sense of foreboding from the minute she stepped into the house. She went upstairs when Castro was looking for something and saw a huddled, frightened figure, half naked and lying on a mattress. It was Michelle.

She tried to flee, but Castro was waiting for her.

Goodbye Amanda.

Amanda's vanishing did send shockwaves through the community. She was, after all, still a teenager and was judged by those whose job it is in the media and the police to gauge value – news-wise, resource-wise – to be a person worthy of expending maximum effort to find. At first, the police considered Amanda to be a runaway, but the FBI soon began to investigate the case as a kidnapping.

The Cleveland *Plain Dealer* newspaper would devote acres of newsprint to her cause. Columnist Regina Brett befriended her mother and kept the story alive, vibrant, reminding the community always that hope was omnipresent, particularly in the family. The month after she had gone, Brett wrote:

Her daughter has been missing for 20 days. Mandy's fate hinges on whoever picked her up from work. Her last words to her family were spoken to her sister on a cellphone, around 7:45 p.m. April 21, as Mandy left her job at Burger King. 'I've got a ride. I'll call you back.' Mandy's mom repeats it over and over, as if she'll find a hidden clue. Who gave her the ride? Where did the driver take her? Is Mandy safe?

Louwana can't sleep or eat. She lives on cigarettes and blind faith. Sitting on the couch in a cloud of smoke, she uses the coffee table as a desk, with two phones ready, a stack of business cards from detectives and FBI agents and ashtrays brimming with Doral and Marlboro butts.

'I don't understand where I stand,' she says. The FBI has put to rest rumors that Mandy ran away and is treating the case as a kidnapping. Mandy had a good relationship with her mom and had never run away. She left $100 in her bedroom she saved to get her nails done and buy a new outfit for her birthday party, which was the next day. 'Mandy waited all week for that party,' her mom said. Mandy would never leave for long without her phone charger and clothes to change out of her maroon Burger King top, black jeans, black sneakers and cap. 'All her clothes are here. No way would she leave with her Burger King outfit on,' her mother said, almost smiling. 'I don't know if she's out there being held, I don't know if she's out there laying on the side of the road somewhere,' Louwana said. 'Who gave her that ride?' Louwana believes it was someone Mandy knew, because her daughter wouldn't even stop and give directions to a stranger.

On that, at least, she was on the money.

Regina Brett tapped into the raw emotion of a mother's pain and in doing so turned Amanda from an abstract statistic into a real person. She became everyone's daughter, everyone's nightmare – especially when that nightmare was compounded, just one week after she vanished, when someone called Louwana on Amanda's cellphone.

'This leads us to believe she was not a runaway,' said FBI agent Robert Hawk. 'Someone had control of her cellphone.' According to agent Hawk, the caller told her mother, 'I have Amanda. She's fine and will be coming home in a couple of days.' The caller sounded like a man between eighteen and thirty years of age, Hawk said.

Louwana said that she asked the caller if she could speak to her daughter. 'I asked to speak to her, and he hung up,' she said.

Cleveland police asked Louwana to keep back part of

the telephone conversation from the public domain. No one, of course, at this time even knew of the existence of Ariel Castro, let alone as a suspect in kidnappings. Amanda was his 'special one' – his chosen one, in his twisted logic – and he felt the need to share it. His grotesque ego did not allow empathy for Amanda's fretting mother to cloud his vision of an idyllic future together. 'I think I said something . . . that I have her daughter and that she's OK and that she's my wife now – something like that, you know, probably not the exact words,' Castro would tell investigators many years later as he recounted his crimes and, in doing so, attempted to justify them. The connection was brief and Louwana was left staring into the phone receiver and the great, dark void her life had become.

But Louwana never gave up hope. She walked the route that her daughter was to walk home on the day before her birthday, to keep her in the news. She continued to be the source of Regina Brett's columns. She laboured under the worst affliction that can befall any mother – not knowing what had happened to her child. So great was her suffering that, after managing to pressure *America's Most Wanted* into airing a segment on Amanda in 2004, which instantaneously reached millions of viewers, she also enlisted the dubious 'aid' of a psychic on the *Montel Williams Show*. The woman told her that Amanda was dead and probably 'in water'. The callous medium, Sylvia Browne, described a short, stocky Burger King customer in his twenties wearing a red fleece coat. Browne went on, 'She's not alive, honey. Your daughter's not the kind who wouldn't call. You will only see your daughter in heaven, on the other side.'

The news crushed Louwana, who walked away from the studio crestfallen and depressed. The grieving mother gave away her daughter's computer and took down her pictures, saying, 'I'm not even buying my baby a Christmas present this year.' She said she believed '98 per cent' in what the psychic said on the show, adding, 'It seems like the God-honest truth. My daughter would always call home.'

The FBI rubbished Browne but, at Louwana's request, agents investigating Amanda's disappearance met with her after the show to discuss Browne's other psychic views on the case. Browne said she envisioned Amanda's jacket in a dumpster with 'DNA on it'.

FBI special agent Kelly Liberti later said that law enforcement agencies listen to all information from all sources, 'but do not employ or seek the assistance of psychics'.

The hunt would go on, but the damage had been done to the frail spirit of Louwana Miller. She died at the age of forty-four, from heart failure and a host of other ailments, a little more than a year after her televised encounter with Sylvia Browne. In a tribute column to her, Regina Brett wrote:

The last time we spoke, she demanded, 'I want her on the news. She's faded away from the whole world. It just kills me. This is killing me.'

It finally did. Regina Brett's column continued:

The psychic said Mandy died on her birthday, that she didn't suffer, that her black hooded jacket was in a dumpster with DNA on it. The psychic promised, 'You'll see her in heaven.' That was Louwana's final hope. Around Christmas I heard Louwana was in the hospital. It still shocked me when she died Thursday. I couldn't help thinking of how she took the faded yellow ribbons off the front-yard fence, washed them and put them on Mandy's bed. How she cried, 'No one cares.' The truth is no one cared as much as she did. No one could. She was a mother facing a fate worse than death: not knowing. Every time I called the FBI, special agent Bob Hawk, who has since retired, would tell me, 'We are working on it every day. We haven't given up.' Louwana did. She died of heart failure.

Her death did not diminish the searches and the praying and the hope. The fliers still went up, the candles were still lit, Amanda's father and other relatives continued trying to keep her name in the spotlight. In July 2012 investigators, acting on a tip from a convicted murderer called Robert Wolford, began to dig up an empty lot at the corner of Wade and West 30th Street, near the Interstate 90 freeway.

Prosecutor Bill Mason said Wolford, aged twenty-six and serving a lengthy prison sentence for murder at the Chillicothe Correctional Institution, wrote to his office indicating that Amanda was buried there and that another man, wanted by the law, was involved in her abduction. 'I probably get letters like this at least once a week from somebody, somewhere, saying something about crime. Some of them lead to something, and most of them don't.'

After digging for forty-eight hours and using dogs trained to sniff out human remains, the forensics specialists were able to tell the family that Wolford was a fantasist and that, wherever Amanda might be, she was certainly nowhere near this particular patch of real estate. In 2009 the Fond du Lac County Sheriff's Office in Wisconsin believed a frozen corpse found by deer hunters had similarities to Amanda. A DNA test with hair taken from a brush at Amanda's home soon ruled this out.

There was a strange twist to the hunt for the phantom body in Cleveland. Pedro Castro, who was briefly a suspect after his brother's discovery in May 2013, was actually filmed for the Fox TV network at the time the digging was going on. Sitting on the stoop of a friend's house, wearing a floral shirt and sunglasses, Castro gestured to the lot and told reporters that looking for Miss Berry's body was 'a waste of money'. The house was just two blocks from 2207, the place where she really was.

In the frenzy that followed the freeing of the girls, there was speculation that Pedro had some kind of insider knowledge – especially as, for a few hours at least, both he and Onil were regarded as co-conspirators with their brother in his diabolical plot. But now it seems that his words were the ramblings of a lonely drunkard, suddenly finding himself with a Warhol moment on prime-time TV. Given that he has been absolved of any involvement in the kidnapping and prolonged incarceration of the women, his was a throwaway remark – in the worst possible taste – but a random comment, nonetheless.

Victim number three of the bizarre 'family' Ariel Castro was building in his home was taken on her way home from Wilbur Wright Middle School, almost exactly a year after Amanda had been taken and nearly two years since Michelle had vanished. Incredibly, she was the best friend of Castro's daughter Arlene, and was a regular on the school bus that he drove. The pair were walking home together when Georgina DeJesus asked Arlene if she would like to come over to her house.

Arlene later said, 'She [Gina] gave me fifty cents to call my mom – and my mom said no, I can't go over to her house. So I told her, and Gina said OK and just walked.'

But Gina now had a problem: she didn't have enough money left for the bus fare to take her home. Yet there was no problem at all. For who should come along but Arlene's dad? That cool musician guy, with some merengue music playing on his car radio.

Only he didn't just happen to be passing by.

He had seen that his daughter was walking with her friend and that they had parted ways. He eased his Toyota car alongside Gina. 'Hey, Gina,' he called. 'You know where I can find Arlene? Can you help me look for her?'

She was in.

She told him how she had lost a quarter phoning Arlene's home and didn't have enough money left for the bus fare.

'No worries, sugar, I can take you home. Just got to spin by my place first, OK?'

At West 105th Street and Lorain Avenue in Cleveland, between 2:45 p.m. and 3:00 p.m. on 2 April 2004, she was gone.

Goodbye Gina.

Gina DeJesus' family and the Castro clan were from the same part of Puerto Rico, went to the same Cleveland clubs, drank in the same bars, shopped in the same supermarkets, bought the same Latino newspapers and formed part of the great Hispanic community which called the city home. Gina's family would later say they 'practically grew up' with the Castros.

Gina DeJesus' great-uncle Noel Ruiz Sr. said the two families used to throw parties at the Caribe Grocery owned by Castro's uncle, at the end of Seymour Avenue. 'Ariel would be at them too,' he said. 'Everyone knows everyone in the Puerto Rican community.'

Members of the Castro and DeJesus families also mingled at the fourteenth birthday party for Gina, a day before she disappeared in 2004. At school Gina was tight with Arlene and another girl called Kayla Rogers. The trio hung out together so much that other pupils nicknamed them 'The Three Musketeers'.

'They were the best of the best of the best of friends,' said Lupe Collins, whose daughter was also friends with the girls. 'Kayla and Arlene and Georgina, they were tight, they really were like three musketeers, no exaggeration. They wouldn't leave each other's sight.'

Kayla and Gina first met in elementary school, and they both befriended Arlene in middle school. They would often go to each other's homes to listen to Spanish music and rap and practise their dance moves. Gina was almost certainly in the Castro home while the other women were imprisoned, although mostly they met at Gina's bigger house on West 71st Street near Clark Avenue.

'We used to hang out on Gina's porch,' said Kayla. 'We had a couple of sleepovers. We would chat on the phone and talk about boys. Yeah, we were gossips. Gossip girls! I used to see Arlene's father, as he worked as a school bus driver. He was my bus driver, also. He'd wink at me and . . . ugh! He would look at us in his mirror and wink.' Kayla, now twenty-three, went on, 'I seem to remember that he used to like light-skinned girls.'

Another girl on the route, Quila Branche, now twenty-two, said, 'He was weird . . . he had a selected few girls he liked. He loved his white girls and his Puerto Rican girls. Girls with long, pretty hair.'

Girls like Gina, who had long, lustrous hair that she often wore in a ponytail and which, people remembered, Castro had on more than one occasion complimented her on.

The close bond between Gina and Arlene was undoubtedly a key factor in Castro choosing to take her. He knew her strengths, he knew her weaknesses and he knew she would not say no to the father of her best pal when the day came for her to slot into his master plan. Gina was just thirty blocks from home when she vanished in an urban area that seemed to be morphing into a concrete Bermuda Triangle for young women. Her mother, Nancy Ruiz, and her father, Felix DeJesus, adored her. They knew of her friendship with Arlene and never for once suspected that the father of a girl they treated as one of their own could ever be behind the disappearance of their beloved daughter. Gina, who was a special-needs pupil at her school – 'slow', as the average, non-expert person would have described her – was a popular teenager, a girl who, along with music and dancing, liked rollerskating and basketball. Her bedroom was festooned with posters of sport and pop stars. She liked jewellery, dancing and confided in her diary that she wanted to marry, have a big family and one day live by the sea.

The FBI immediately joined in the hunt for the missing girl. While the linkage had been tentatively made between her disappearance and that of Amanda, Michelle Knight was not linked to the duo. She would continue to be classified as a 'walkaway' – an adult who had left because of a grievance with the system which took away her child. But the disappearance of Amanda and Gina demanded more scrutiny, especially as Wright Middle School was just over half a mile away from where Amanda Berry had disappeared a year earlier. Forty-eight hours after the police were first called about Gina, the Feds were in on the case.

'They offered their assistance and we took them up on it,' said Cleveland police lieutenant Brian Heffernan.

That first Sunday, as Felix and Nancy began stapling the first missing posters of their daughter to telegraph poles and fence posts in the locality, the FBI agents were moving among the locals, asking questions, trying to map out a pattern, an MO, anything which might give them a break. Gina's bedroom was forensically searched, the agents looking for love notes or clues to secret boyfriends who might hold the key to the mystery of her vanishing. Police even brought dogs to search her neighbourhood, but nothing turned up. The security-camera videotapes from four stores on Lorain and Clark Avenues yielded zero images of potential suspects when scrutinized frame by frame.

Nothing.

The search for Gina followed the same pattern as that for Amanda – but with added impetus, given that both went missing in the same area. Police officers from Cleveland and the Regional Transit Authority searched desolate areas and parks, using dogs and heat-seeking scanners. Police officers joined city and school district officials at a packed meeting of locals shortly after Gina failed to return home, aware that, each day Gina and Amanda remained unaccounted for, the pressure mounted.

'We have followed up on every possible lead we have and we will continue to do so,' Mayor Jane Campbell told the crowd of nearly 500 people. 'We still do not have a grip on where Gina is. We have to have every bit of information.'

While some locals were pleased at the seriousness with which the authorities seemed to be taking the girls' disappearance, there were also deep levels of frustration over the handling of other unsolved disappearances – most notably Amanda's – in the neighbourhood. Police had to usher several people out of the hall as they heckled the mayor. Those who had seemingly walked off beyond the horizon, never to be seen again, included Cordell Sheperd, aged thirty-seven, a black man who vanished in January 2004, Noel Morris, aged fifty-one, who went missing two years earlier, Jonni Perkins, aged fifty, who disappeared in 2001, and Michael Hodge, aged forty-nine, who also went missing in 2004. During the time the women were in captivity, a seventeen-year-old girl called Ashley Summers went missing in 2007. She disappeared in the same neighbourhood as Castro's victims and has never been found.

Despite these disappearances, there was nothing to suggest that Cleveland was different from any other city in the USA. It wasn't until Amanda and Gina went missing that people felt an element of fear. They began to believe there really was a predator in their midst.

The police started to pour more resources into the hunt for Gina and Amanda. Some twenty-five sheriff's deputies tracked down offenders living in Gina's neighbourhood who were wanted on warrants for sex crimes, and seven arrests followed.

'We're just trying to shake some trees and see if we can get any information,' said Chief Deputy Charles Corrao. 'I'm personally tired of these animals taking our children.'

Information about Gina was sent electronically to the National Center for Missing and Exploited Children, which posted Gina's photo on its website where she was listed as an 'endangered runaway'. Another group called 'A Child Is Missing' placed 2,700 calls to random homes within a half-mile radius of Gina's home in a bid to elicit information about her. Had anybody seen her? Did anybody know of paedophiles in the area? Had anyone seen anything suspicious? All information gained was later passed on to the police, who made tours of local schools, speaking at assemblies to ask pupils if anyone had seen anything or could tell them anything about Gina.

'The information to be gathered is of prime importance,' said Cleveland schools chief executive officer Barbara Byrd-Bennett.

There was a glimmer of good news, if it could be called that. The police determined that there was no sign or suspicion that any violence had been levelled at the missing girl when she vanished. Commander Gary Gingell, who headed the investigation, confirmed that police were also looking into a separate kidnapping and rape case 'to see if there are connections'. On 22 March of that year, a teenaged girl reported that a man grabbed her as she waited for the bus near West 40th Street and Denison Avenue. The girl told police the man sexually assaulted her, then dropped her off. That man was described as white, about twenty-five years old, six feet tall and about 200 pounds.

This, of course, was a false lead and nothing like the physique of the real perpetrator of the crime.

Gina's parents' home became a shrine to her memory, a place where friends and relatives and casual strangers alike dropped in to offer words of comfort and solace.

The mayor was one of them, saying, 'We have but one goal – to bring her back home safely.'

Gina prayer meetings were held at local churches. The posters bearing her image and that of Amanda sprouted like the weeds which grew in the abandoned lots peppering the neighbourhood. But, according to *The Plain Dealer*, inside her home hope was diminishing. The longer that time went on without a resolution:

. . . family members are sinking into despair. Gina's father, Felix, is 'beyond desperate' to bring her home, Gina's cousin Sylvia Colon said. Police and FBI agents continue to investigate, but no new information has surfaced. Authorities are offering a $20,000 reward for details that lead to Gina or missing teen Amanda Berry, another girl who disappeared on the west side more than a year ago. 'We're still committed, most definitely,' FBI Special Agent Bob Hawk said, 'but we have nothing of any value right now.' Felix DeJesus is frustrated and worries that authorities are giving up on his daughter. He looks for Gina every evening after work, sometimes accompanied by relatives or community activists. 'I will not give up,' he said recently, sitting in his living room. 'As long as she's out there missing, I'm going to be out there with her.' DeJesus said police have asked him to stop going out at night to search. But Gina's sister Mayra said the searches are crucial. Searchers meet different people at night, Mayra DeJesus said, and are approached by some who have tips. Family members pass them along to the FBI.

Often, the family reviews Gina's case, leafing through a booklet of sexual offenders living in the area and hunting for missed clues that might bring Gina home. But the volunteer efforts can lead to trouble. On May 3 that year Felix DeJesus was accused with other men of breaking down the apartment door of a sexual offender living near West 104th Street and Lorain Avenue. Gina disappeared a block away on April 2. DeJesus denied he had anything to do with the broken door. Authorities said at the time it was unlikely he would be charged, but the possibility concerned and angered him. He said police told him they planned to watch him. 'I'm not a bad person,' he said. 'I'm not a vigilante. I'm desperate to find my daughter. It hurts so much.'

At one point in the hunt, police scoured the home of

Matthew Hurayt, a 35-year-old registered sex criminal. They had received a tip-off that Gina's body was buried under the garage of his home. Both he and a man called John McDonough, who lived at Hurayt's house, were arrested on suspicion of aggravated murder but were freed after a night in jail when searchers found neither bodies nor live human beings at the premises.

'We're disappointed that the search wasn't as fruitful as we hoped,' police lieutenant Thomas Stacho said. 'But we would have been remiss if we didn't investigate this lead.' He said that after receiving the tip, investigators were 'morally and ethically' obligated to conduct the search.

For Gina's father, and her mother, the hunt would drag on for many long years to come.

The family members of the missing girls clung to the hope that their loved ones were safe and well. None were aware that all three girls had willingly stepped into the car of a man they knew, albeit not extremely well, but at least someone who emanated an aura of trust and reliability, whose demeanour suggested that no harm would come to them if they went off with him. This was a key side to the Janus personality of Castro as gatekeeper. He could do plausibility, affability and emit signals of trust as and when he chose. It was one of the first things that he said to police after he was arrested: 'I did not force anyone to come into my car and into my house. They came in because they wanted to. That was their mistake.'

And this was true. It was their mistake to take at face value the smiling, sunny Ariel Castro, who was regarded by his bandmates and by neighbours on Seymour Avenue as one of the better people on a low-grade block heading south by the day. They could not know, as they accepted his ride home and the casual invitation to step inside his house, of the horrors that were about to be unleashed. What psychiatrists want to discover is why the plan evolved in the way it did. Why did his sexual obsessions drive him to keep on adding women into a house that wasn't soundproofed, where he could have been exposed at any time by a nosy neighbour or an inquisitive cop?

Behavioural expert and criminal defence attorney Darren Kavinoky spoke to the author of this book about the forces driving Castro and why he was so confident that he could get away with things for as long as he did. An on-air legal analyst and a special correspondent for the syndicated show *omg! Insider*, where he reports on legal, political, and pop-culture issues, Mr Kavinoky said Castro had one important accomplice in his crimes – his neighbourhood.

'It's a high crime area. People don't want to get involved. You have a house with sheeting on the windows which, was it in a "good" 'hood, would mean you are going to have questions asked. You are going to attract attention, you are going to attract stares, you may even attract a police officer knocking on the door to ask if anything is wrong. But where he was, no one thought it was out of the ordinary. You know, Fritzl in Austria who sealed up his daughter, and the guy Priklopil who kidnapped the girl to make her love him, they displayed a lot more criminal cunning than Castro. They created underground dungeons with time locks and secret entrances. Castro was essentially a low-rent operator in a low-rent community who did what he did because he thought he could get away with it. And you know what? He did. I am horrified by what he did, his crimes were heinous, but I am not surprised. I think in the society we live in, where people look away, that there are probably, sadly, many more girls like the ones who were found at 2207 Seymour Avenue, Cleveland, Ohio.

'There is a show on American TV called *What Would You Do?* in which secret cameras record the actions of people in situations that require a certain amount of moral action, moral courage. Actors will, say, pretend to be drunk while loading children into a car and then get behind the wheel to drive away. Or a man will hit a woman on a busy street in full view of passers-by. The cameras record what happens next. While there are certainly people of strong character and convictions out there, often people turn away, walk away, don't want to get involved, and there was a large amount of that going on with Castro. Who asked questions when a single guy who lives alone is taking McDonald's meals for four back to his house? Who asked questions when the daughter was born to him – who she really was – when he paraded her around the neighbourhood? His power complex gave him the smarts to recognize that he could command the situation, and he did. I believe, in that house, he was working through his own family torments in his cruel treatment of the women under his spell. He created a family, but it was one in his own warped image.'

A psychiatric specialist working in Los Angeles, who asked not to be named because of the work she does with the institutionalized criminally insane on behalf of the State of California, said in another interview for this book that she believed the libido which drove Castro was working in tandem with two other forces: a desire for utter control, because he had so little of it in his own pathetic life, and the desire for a family unit, which Mr Kavinoky referred to.

'Taking his libido first, he clearly has an extreme sex drive. I saw the comments of the prosecutor in the Fritzl case in Austria, which declared that as long as he [Josef Fritzl] had a libido he would remain a danger to women. I certainly believe that to be the case with Castro. He lacked the courage, or was too smart, to become a street rapist, which would have entailed too much danger, too many risks of being caught, too much loose DNA rolling around. So, like Fritzl, he decides he wants what some call shelf-and-stack sex; women he has turned into objects that he can pleasure himself upon before putting them back into the compartments he has created for them, both physically and in his mind. The second, which perhaps should be the first, compulsion that drives him is his need for control. It is overarching. I have seen reports that he sometimes screamed abuse at the small children he was in charge of on his bus, which gives some indication as to how bad he must feel about himself inside that he needs a terrified child to be in awe of him.

'This need to control, I would surmise, was nurtured in him as a child, probably as an impotent rage against spousal abuse (possibly seeing his mother being hit by his father) and which has been channelled since then into a hatred of women because none of them measured up to the caring mother who soothed him, indulged him, made things better for him after he had seen such abuse. Castro is too arrogant to believe himself a rapist. He does not see himself as the stranger in a balaclava leaping out of a bush. He is an undereducated, emotionally unstable man isolated by his own fantasies. Unable to form proper relationships with women (perhaps rebuffed too many times during the strains of adolescence) he has a personality, I would suggest, that has virtually zero empathy for others – classic psychopathic behaviour. He will also, I believe, have high testosterone levels, driving him on. Everything and everyone must be subsumed to his and his needs alone. He would have held to the belief that his victims got what they got because they were "asking" for it – by getting into his car, by going into his house, by showing him the respect he demanded (notwithstanding that that respect was given at the end of a chain and through violence).

'He will have had utterly no remorse for the emotional trauma he will have caused his victims that can be worse than any physical injury. Women who are raped have nightmares, panic attacks, waves of self-doubt, an overwhelming sense of distrust. These are the smashed bricks of their lives that therapists will have to work with to try to rebuild his victims. The lives of women who are raped are for ever changed. Many say they will never be the same, that it is like dying. Rapists choose those who are vulnerable to rape, and all of these women, in their own way, were vulnerable when they were kidnapped.

'But Castro would not have recognized this. Fritzl, at his trial in 2009 and whose case is now de rigueur for anyone who studies sex criminals and the torments which motivate them, told the court that he believed, after initially forcing himself upon his own daughter, that she acquiesced and slipped into the fantasy role he had created for her in his mind – sex goddess put upon earth to serve him and his attendant fantasies, for ever and ever, amen. It is likely that in the bizarre housey-housey set-up that Ariel Castro constructed in Cleveland he convinced himself that he had created a nuclear family, one which was there because they liked his discipline, liked his lovemaking (he would never call it rape) and liked the set-up. His arrogance would have blinded him to their pain and misery.

'I think this figure of three was significant. Again, from what I have read – and I have had no access to any psychiatric reports on either him or the women under his control for all this time – I would say that each one had a unique function. Michelle Knight, the one he abused most and allegedly beat until she miscarried (rapists like him never consider birth control) was the unfortunate Cinderella, the "punching bag" as the media have called her. An unmarried mother, he would have categorized her in his mind as little better than a prostitute. Amanda Berry, however, was entirely different. Although raped and abused like all the others, this was the one he placed on a pedestal, the one he deemed worthy of his seed. The only one, in fact, he allowed to carry her pregnancy through to birth. And the third captive, Gina, may have fulfilled one of two roles. That of another daughter (even though he raped her) or perhaps, in his planning, she was the one who he would continue to keep on if the other two, in his view, became "expendable". This radical solution must have run through his mind, as it ran through the mind of Fritzl as his cellar children grew up and he grew older. Remember, first, last and always, the needs of Ariel Castro were paramount at all times. This was never about them. He wanted a family, he got a family, period. Only his skewed moral barometer would decide what was "normal" and what was not in that house.'

And as Dr Michael Ghiglieri, an Arizona biologist who has written extensively about male violence, explained, 'The fact is testosterone is a real kick-starter for violence. It's a kick-starter for every male trait, not just violence. It is the responsible hormone for making males. It does affect behaviour, it actually forces aggressive behaviour. Of course, as humans we do have the choice as individuals whether we are aggressive or not. But the fact is testosterone does affect male attitudes and the propensities to violence.

'I think, in general, if you want to get the simplest perspective on it, males use violence to control females, and they do it very often, and they control those females for sexual reasons. It's done in every species.' He cites a ten-year study looking at more than a million cases of rape in the USA. 'It's unfortunately a huge sample of victims,' he says, 'and it turns out that 88 per cent of these women are between the ages of twelve and twenty-eight. Three-quarters of all victims fell between the ages of eighteen and twenty-five. So rapists are seeking the women that men everywhere are seeking.'

Just like Ariel Castro did.

4. Welcome to Hell, Bitch

The road map to hell is a bland document. The criminal indictment against Ariel Castro detailing some of his crimes allows no real glimpse into the terror, the horror of his brutal reign over three innocent women. Within its pages terrible transgressions are chronicled in the dusty argot of prosecutors. Yet for Michelle, Amanda and Gina the descent into hell began soon enough.

None of the women have yet spoken publicly of their ordeals, save for a short TV address after they gained their freedom to say they had suffered, were now grateful to be free and were moving on. Detectives and therapists, as well as their closest family members have, so far, been the sharers of their terrible secrets. They have stories to tell for which they have been offered many hundreds of thousands of dollars – dollars which they will need for their future lives, ongoing medical treatment and homes of their own. All three women have pledged to remain silent until justice has run its course against their tormentor, for fear of prejudicing his trial. What follows here is based on the insight of investigators, on what authorities have revealed about the women's time in captivity and what the brevity of the language used in the indictment actually meant in terms of fear, pain and blood for the unwilling dwellers at 2207 Seymour Avenue.

Because of what happened to Natascha Kampusch and to Elisabeth Fritzl and her cellar children in Austria we are able to fathom some of the anxieties Castro's captives faced and the coping strategies they developed to overcome them. But we were not there when babies were beaten from the womb of Michelle, nor when she was chained to a pole in Castro's terrifying basement torture chamber, nor when similar indignities were heaped on her fellow inmates. Empathy – the singular human quality missing from the flawed mind of Ariel Castro – is what is needed to comprehend what he did to these young women in that house during those times.

What must have Michelle thought when she walked into the grimy front room of Ariel Castro's, believing she was only going to stop for a few minutes on her way home? 'Shorty', as she was known among her friends – she is only 4 feet 7 inches tall – would have noticed the empty fast-food cartons sprawled among the instruments and music sheets littering the room. The light would have been filtered by the heavy plastic sheeting tacked over the windows – what was *that* all about? – and she would probably have spotted the padlocks hanging on the doors.

'Can't be too careful these days, sugar,' joked the monster, 'what with all these criminals about.'

And then it began.

Michelle was bludgeoned and dragged upstairs to what would become her cell. Later the same day, he tied her and frogmarched her down into the basement where he had installed a pole which ran from the ceiling to the floor and was held in place by steel bolts.

The following day, in the language of the indictment:

> [Castro] did engage in sexual conduct, to wit: sexual intercourse with Jane Doe 1 by purposely compelling her to submit by force or threat of force (first sexual assault of Jane Doe 1).

The rape torture had started. It would continue for Michelle for almost eleven more years.

She was left naked, shackled to the pole, throughout that long first night. He had punched her repeatedly in the head and there were bruises all over her body. A small window in the basement was lined with the same dark plastic sheeting as she had seen in the living room and was overlaid with wooden board and chicken wire. She could hear the tyres of cars squelching on the hot asphalt outside, but she made no sound: Castro had told her that to do so would result in another beating and a gag.

Michelle, easily confused at the best of times in normal situations, was overwhelmed by what had befallen her. This was a man who drove a bus for schoolkids. He was taking her home. How did she end up here? In her panic and terror she began to have visions in the damp, earth-smelling cellar where mould grew on the walls and the cold seeped into her bones. Hers was a loneliness usually only experienced by captured soldiers or convicts in solitary confinement – but at least they might be expected to anticipate such eventualities because of the lives they chose to lead. She was an innocent, lost in the grip of emotions she could neither understand nor control.

Castro visited her repeatedly over the next week – it may have been longer, but Michelle lost track of time in the darkness. He always switched off the light when he left, and the little light she received through the blocked window was deceptive. She never knew if it was dawn or dusk, or if a street light was shining through. She had a bucket for a toilet and a bottle of water. Her jailer brought food down to her in the brown carry-out bags he'd received from takeaway restaurants. Invariably she gnawed at half a burger or a few chicken wings he had not been able to finish. All the while, in between this degradation, he raped her and he beat her. Like Fritzl, Castro did not bother with contraception. For him to have done so would have cost money he could ill afford. And besides, it would have somehow infringed upon his own narcissistic vision of himself as the macho, virile gatekeeper of this secret world. Anyhow, he had another way of dealing with this bitch should she ever fall pregnant.

After around ten days Michelle was bound by the wrists one morning and dragged upstairs. Castro threw her into a room subdivided from another bedroom by sheetrock plaster. The window was blacked out like all the others.

'Be good and you can listen to TV and radio,' he said. 'Fuck me around and you know what you will get.'

He allowed her to clean up in the small bathroom on the ground floor – the only one in the house – and she was grateful for this.

Grateful. The bonding of one captive spirit to the force which bound it had begun. Michelle was thankful for small mercies, which experts know is how the power is maintained in such corrupt relationships. Self-esteem, pride, anger, rationality – all are eroded like cliffs at the edge of powerful seas. Until all that is left is pliable, mouldable clay. The process of the disintegration of Michelle's spirit was rapidly under way.

Stronger victims, like Elisabeth Fritzl and, later in that same Cleveland house, Amanda Berry, were able to practise something mind doctors call disassociation, the mental exercise of imagining that what is happening to you is actually happening to someone else. Victims speak of rising above themselves when being raped, to observe the attack taking place upon a mythical other. This detachment is a defence mechanism of the mind – the separation of the body from the brain – allowing victims to get through one more terrible attack, one more gruesome day.

Unfortunately, Michelle was intellectually incapable of such psychological gymnastics. She cried, he beat her, she cried again and he beat her some more, crushing blows to the face and head that would ultimately deform her jaw and damage her hearing. But he was, he convinced himself, slowly taming the bitch. He did so by taunting her that she was worthless, a nut job who had had her child taken from her, a slut who slept with all the boys at school and who was so 'loose' that she deserved the gang rape which had befallen her.

'Ain't no one looking for you, sugar,' he said to her. 'You're gone. You're mine now. Daddy will take good care of you.'

*

In her book about her time in captivity, *3,096 Days*, Natascha Kampusch wrote how she became 'grateful' to Priklopil for allowing her to go swimming in the forest and other concessions:

> I was immeasurably grateful to the kidnapper for such small pleasures. I still am. Back then, I clung to even the tiniest human gesture, because I needed to see goodness in a world in which I could change nothing. Within the evil, at least brief moments of normality were possible. One day, I even told him: 'I forgive you, because everyone makes mistakes sometimes.' In a sense, the man who'd stolen me, who'd taken my family and identity away from me, became my new 'family'. His psychopathic fantasies became my reality.

But Priklopil, deviant and abnormal though he was – he used food to try to control his captive and often beat her hideously when she upset him – did have a bizarre sort of love for Natascha. That was his game plan: to take a young, impressionable girl, seal her off from her family and the world she used to know, and slowly, over time, convince her to love him. The love *was* there, strange though it may have been. For Michelle, there never was any.

She was an object – objectified from day one.

Elizabeth Smart is another high-profile kidnap victim uniquely placed to understand what Michelle and, later, the other women went through. She was taken from her bedroom in Salt Lake City, Utah, in June 2002, aged fourteen. The abduction was witnessed by her sister, Mary

Katherine, who shared her room. Her kidnapper was Brian David Mitchell, who worked for the family doing odd jobs and called himself 'Emmanuel'.

He took Elizabeth to his home in the town of Sandy, where he and his wife, Wanda Barzee, tormented their victim. Thanks to Mary Katherine's testimony, Mitchell emerged as a leading suspect in the case. When he and his wife were spotted, in March 2003, with Elizabeth – dressed in a grey wig, sunglasses and veil – the schoolgirl was rescued and returned to her parents. Her kidnapper is currently serving life in prison, while Barzee was sentenced to fifteen years. Ms Smart has since become a leading advocate for missing persons, and last year married Scottish-born Matthew Gilmour after meeting him when they were both serving as Mormon missionaries in Paris.

She said the rapes she endured at Mitchell's hands made her feel worthless. She said the traditional religious values she was raised with – values shared by the Cleveland captives – also made her feel worthless. 'You feel that as you have lost your purity you are no longer worthy of love. I'll never forget how I felt, lying there on the ground, the first time he assaulted me. I felt like my soul had been crushed. I felt like I wasn't even human any more. How could anybody love me, or want me or care about me? I have nothing but respect and admiration for these women for what they endured.'

And no one endured more than Michelle. The language of hatred, of disrespect for all women, was a central plank of Castro's philosophy. All his life, as his friends have testified for this book, women shunned him when he presented his 'charming' side to them at dances and bars. Those who said no to him were wearing short dresses and high heels – therefore, in his mind, they were 'asking for it'. The fact that they rejected him meant they were obviously 'getting it' elsewhere, therefore they were sluts and whores. Later, it made him feel good about himself to demean the object of his desire, and the 'dirty talk' he poured out when violating Michelle was essential to his power and control. By reducing her, he enlarged himself.

Feminist author Erin Riordan said, 'The word "slut" sucks. So do "whore", "ho" and "trashy". These words are all feminized terms, and they are words that are used to punish women who enjoy sex. Historically, sex has never been about women. Women, until very recent history, and even now in many parts of the world, were considered property, owned by their fathers and then their husbands. Prior to the business transaction that transferred a woman from father to husband, women were expected to be virgins.'

Because she was not a virgin, because she was a woman, and because she would have rejected him in any normal social situation for the pathetic half-man he really was, Castro considered Michelle to be a whore for the taking, and treated her as such.

Inevitably, it happened – a pregnancy – and it is documented for the first time on pages eight and nine in the indictment:

The Grand Jurors on their oath further find that the Defendant unlawfully, on or about September 1 2002 to

December 31 2002, did by force, threat or deception purposely remove Jane Doe 1 from the place where she was
found or restrain the liberty of her for the purpose of
engaging in sexual activity with Jane Doe 1 against her
will. (The restraint associated with the conception of
Jane Doe 1 first pregnancy.)

The dates refer to an attack in which Michelle was
shackled early on, but the first pregnancy did not occur
until late in 2006, shortly before Amanda was due to give
birth. This was something that was not in Castro's master
plan, and certainly not with her.

An investigator close to the case said, 'From the get-go
it was clear that Michelle was the punching bag, the one
who bore the brunt of his fury. She was, in his mind, his
"pliable prostitute", intellectually and morally way below
the salt at his table. He insulted her for being "backward"
and "deranged" because she had lost custody of her child.
He nurtured fantasies of fathering more children after
scarring the lives of his first brood with Grimilda Figueroa.
But Michelle Knight was not part of those plans. She was
a "comfort girl" who was there to attend solely to his sexual needs. When she fell pregnant he could not allow it to
come to term.'

There were never any doctors or nurses called to the
house during the time Michelle, or the others, were held
against their will. Medication came in the form of
over-the-counter prescriptions, low-grade painkillers and
headache tablets. Castro would never risk his scheme
being blown apart by taking anyone to a clinic for

treatment, and certainly not for an abortion. There was only one thing for it.

Alone, back in that cellar, her head muffled by a motor-cycle helmet, he strapped her to what he termed the 'punishment pole' and beat her. Then he put her on a tea-only diet for several days, made her perform knee bends and jumping-jack exercises so she would miscarry. He kicked her and he stomped with all his weight on her stomach.

According to Michelle, he would do it three more times, when her periods stopped and her breasts began to swell. Afterwards, he would make her clean up the residue of what had been a child forming inside her, while he listened to salsa music or watched the Cleveland baseball team, the Indians, on TV.

It was no big deal.

Not to a guy whose emotional wiring burned out long ago.

Castro, fuelled by years of frustration and pornography, used Michelle as a lab rat before the others arrived. He raped her in the small bathroom downstairs, he raped her upstairs in her 'cell', he took her out to the garage and raped her there. He even raped her inside one of his vans, with her hands shackled to the passenger grips. Over time her poor diet began to take its toll on her small frame. Lack of vitamins in a diet of low-grade junk food, tinned meat and soup lead to gum problems, skin problems, nose bleeds. Never fat, she lost weight, became lethargic, suffered gingivitis and a deficit of vitamins A, C, D and E. The lack of sunlight caused her skin to fade to a ghostly white pallor.

With weakness came a greater reliance on the captor

who, even in her acquiescence to his will, continued to abuse her on a horrific scale. If she did something that rankled or displeased him he would force her into stress positions in the cellar, her hands tied behind her back, hoisted up by her shoulders on to the punishment pole with her feet barely touching the ground, the pain of feeling her shoulders almost – but not quite – dislocating themselves from their sockets driving her to the edge of sanity. Often the 'hanging' punishments were accompanied by her eyes and mouth being sealed with duct tape. Michelle prayed during these torture sessions that her sinuses would stay unblocked and that she could continue to breathe. She could rely on only one thing – that the good moods of her abductor would continue to outweigh the bad ones.

It was in her interest to bow down to him.

This is the quandary of all kidnap victims. Jeffrey Kluger, a senior editor for America's *Time* magazine who oversees the publication's science and technology reporting, wrote of the Cleveland victims:

Abduction is a singularly grotesque transaction. In a single instant, a relationship between two people changes to one of captor and prisoner, owner and chattel. One holds absolute power and the other holds none. Worse, the person in charge knew the moment was coming – sometimes for a long time. The powerless one had no idea.

The head-spinning news out of Cleveland raises questions that we've had to ask too many times before. What happens to the mind of any person – especially a child – after such a trauma? Is full recovery even possible, and if so, how do you achieve it? More puzzling, in the months and sometimes years victims like this are imprisoned, why don't they try to escape when opportunities present themselves? Perhaps the Cleveland women did try: they were discovered when one of the three men who have been accused of kidnapping them, Ariel Castro, left the house where they were held, and Berry began pounding on the door and screaming for a neighbour to rescue her. Maybe this was the only time since her abduction in 2003 that she had such a chance. But in a small house on a crowded block with a kidnapper who was often seen outside, that was probably not the case. Clearly, something breaks the mind and the will of anyone so stripped of autonomy. As much as we might like to tell ourselves that we'd fight like wildcats in the same situation, the chances are pretty good we'd do exactly the same thing they did. The challenge becomes understanding precisely what kind of psychological damage is done to victims in cases like this, partly so we can better fathom the human mind, but much more importantly, so we can help them heal.

The worst part of the Cleveland abductions was that all of the victims were children or teens when they were taken – except for Knight, and she was only twenty. All of them were also girls. As a rule, children's emotional resilience matches their physical resilience, which means they heal faster than adults. But there's a terrible toll on children who grow up in a state of captivity; confinement stunts them at the very moment in their lives they're supposed to be maturing emotionally and intellectually.

What prevented these women from crying out or breaking free whenever they had the chance? It's too glib simply to invoke the go-to 'Stockholm Syndrome', the phenomenon of captives eventually identifying with their captors, and leave it at that. But it's nonetheless a big part of things. At first there is indeed the scratching and fighting and hollering that we all imagine we'd be able to keep up indefinitely. But slowly, victims surrender to powerlessness, something that is accelerated if the kidnapper shows a willingness to inflict pain, but also to withhold it.

Castro had a gun. He would wave it at the victims and say he was not afraid to use it if they even 'thought about thinking' about trying to escape. 'Through a programme of prolonged physical, sexual and psychological violence the defendant was able to keep the victims in a state of powerlessness. He made them believe their physical survival depended on him.' These were the words of the prosecutors when the bill was finally presented to Castro for settlement in full on 1 August 2013 – the day he, not the girls, became a prisoner. For ever.

But that was in a future the victims really believed they might not live to see, and so they tried to gauge his moods, placate him and act subserviently to head off the worst of the violence before it erupted.

'Instead of being tortured, you receive kindness,' says Dr Tina J. Walch, director of ambulatory services at Zucker Hillside Hospital in New Hyde Park, New York. 'You are given a drop of water, you're not beaten. You begin to develop feelings of gratitude. Over time it wears on even the strongest person.

'The human need for affiliation asserts itself too. Being in the physical company of someone – anyone – is better than being utterly alone. If this is your only contact, you come to value that contact, so that even when given the opportunity to run away or get help, you don't. That fact is important for the victims themselves to remember as they recover, in case they ever – as they well might – blame themselves even a little for the years they lost.'

With four small bedrooms, 1,400 square feet of living space, and no air conditioning or central heating, Michelle baked during that first summer of her incarceration in Seymour Avenue, and froze in the winter which followed. Plans of the house, obtained by the American media, show small rectangular rooms, 14 feet across and only 6 feet wide. One room measures a claustrophobic 6 feet by 6 feet. This was Michelle's. There was no bed, just a mattress on the floor. It seems that Castro chained her up during the day but took her chains off at night. As she became ever more institutionalized within his orbit, her jailer would occasionally let her roam the house while he was out, assured that she would not attempt to break out. She didn't. But when Amanda Berry came to join the 'family', things were to be very different – for her, for him, for the dynamic of the house itself.

Amanda came into the Seymour Avenue prison, like Michelle before her, convinced that hers was a moment-ary stopover before continuing home, her mind not really on the here and now, but on tomorrow, and the birthday celebrations she had planned with her friends. Like Michelle, there was no violence, no coercion when she went inside. She entered the house of her own free will and, again, this was an important psychological point for Castro. These, he convinced himself, were not prisoners but willing participants in his grand game.

Yet Amanda was no Michelle. She was an extremely bright, feisty young woman who had not earned her schoolgirl nickname 'Amando Commando' for nothing. Investigators said she tried to escape on the very night she was kidnapped but was caught by Castro before she got out of the door, bludgeoned to the ground. It would be another decade before she would get as close to that door again. At this stage, she did not know of the existence of Michelle on the floor above her. In the language of the indictment:

On or about April 21 2003, the Grand Jurors on their oaths further find that the Defendant unlawfully did engage in sexual conduct, to wit sexual intercourse by purposely compelling her by force or threat of force. (First sexual assault of Jane Doe 2 after she attempted to escape.)

Castro saw he would have to break this one, like he had broken the one before her. The indictment goes on to describe how the suspect tied his victim's legs and mouth with tape before dragging her down the steps into the basement, shackling her to the punishment pole, placing the motorcycle helmet he had used on Michelle over her head and raping her. Amanda was not kept in the cellar for days but was removed to a room upstairs, next to Michelle's, where she was chained to a heater and raped over the coming days. The indictment shows that, with a fresh victim to satisfy Castro's urges, Michelle had a respite.

Castro would wake Amanda at certain times of the day to assault her. He would drive his bus home in the lunch hour and rape her. She, like Michelle, was also raped in the bathroom, the van and the garage, attacks that took place when neighbours were not around to witness anything. On one occasion, before he had 'tamed' her, she fought back and he wrapped a vacuum cleaner cord around her neck and hissed, 'Fight me and I will pull this until your eyes bleed.' She stopped struggling. He raped her again. Curiously, he never beat Amanda the way he assaulted Michelle. She wasn't so special that he couldn't rape her and starve her, but she sensed that he had another purpose for her than being merely a comfort woman.

Castro had, according to police sources, cut small holes in the doors of their locked rooms so that he could slide food in, just as convicts are fed in jail. For weeks, months at a time, the girls were kept in their rooms, fed with the junk that Castro bought on his meagre wages, allowed out to the bathroom, but then ushered back in again. 'The defendant controlled every aspect of the environment in which the victims lived,' prosecutors would later say. 'He controlled the temperature and the inflow of food and drink. He used the cold of the basement and the heat of the attic as punishment techniques. The defendant kept a gun and threatened to shoot them if they ever tried to escape.'

There were locks on their individual doors and

sometimes, just sometimes, he removed them. But the terror he instilled in them bought their compliance.

They did not try to break out.

Contact between the two was not officially allowed. For the first three years they saw only him, but they whispered in the dark and during the daylight hours when he was away. The effect of this solitude was felt in many ways, one of which was hyper-responsivity to external sounds. They could hear a car from half a mile away, a bird singing above the noise of the street, the chatter of people on their stoops as they barbecued food. That was a plus – and one which would stand them in good stead much later – but mostly, the effects were all negative.

They have since talked to carers of being prone to panic attacks, hearing voices inside their heads – often in whispers – and experiencing hallucinations. They have complained of being unable to concentrate on small things as the combined effects of fear and hunger ate away at their souls and their sanity. 'Narcotized,' was how Amanda would describe her feelings after she was freed.

In the jargon of the psychiatrists, they formed what are called 'intrusive obsessional thoughts' with the emergence of 'primitive aggressive ruminations'. In plain English, these amounted to dark thoughts of revenge against their captor. Castro, perhaps sensing that the 'family unit' he was intent on creating was not as comfortable with the notion as he was, supplied them only with plastic cutlery. He also allowed them no access to sharp objects, in case they felt like taking the easy way out by ending their own lives. That was another headache he could do without.

Time in Seymour Avenue was like that in all prisons. Slow time. They had limited access to radio and TV – Amanda saw the efforts of the community in trying to keep her name in the news, nurturing the belief that she was still alive, while Michelle brooded on the apparent lack of attention given to her – but this access was stopped whenever Castro felt they had misbehaved. This included the times he 'tested' them in captivity by removing the chains and leaving the doors to the bedrooms open. During such times, Amanda would sneak in to see Michelle, give her a hug, try to instill hope in her, but she was like a shell-shocked victim from some long-ago war. She stared into the distance, seemingly unaware of who she was or where she was. This torpor would stay with her until the day she was freed. Amanda would test her jailer by prowling downstairs, looking around, only to be surprised when Castro leapt back into the room to deliver a stinging blow around her head. Sometimes the blow would be followed by being tied naked to the punishment pole.

He may not have had much in the way of an effective physical security system, but Castro made up for it with the mind games that forced the 'family' into obedience. He told them there were others who had not made it home.

'Do you wanna be like them?' he asked.

Amanda often asked him, when his mood seemed accessible enough, what he was doing with them.

'You wanted to be here, you came here,' he replied. 'You're mine now. That's your choice and all you need to know.' He would lie, saying that the word on the street was that the searches and the vigils and the prayer meetings were all cosmetic. 'No one really cares about you, baby, 'cept me,' he would say. 'I'm all you've got.'

But as her survival gene kicked in, telling her that resistance was useless, another part of her pledged that she would, one day, overcome all this – the rapes, the bedsores which wept because she spent so long lying down, unable to change position because of the chains that bound her, the humiliations, the stink of urine and faeces in the rooms (they were supplied with plastic toilets and rarely allowed to use the bathroom downstairs) and the starvation. She pledged she would survive.

Ariel Castro made her succumb, but he never broke her.

Soon the tribe was joined by the third and last victim, another friend of the family, this time only fourteen years old and about to receive a sharp lesson in mankind's ability to descend into darkness. Tricked, like the other two, into the house, she sensed something was wrong as Castro fussed and made excuses. She turned to leave and he was upon her, smothering her with a pillow to stifle a scream. He bound her and took her into the bathroom where he pawed her all over, with the other captives just feet away upstairs in their rooms. The indictment says he clawed at her breasts and then her vagina before tiring of seeing himself, the master, reflected back from the dirty wall mirror. He bound her and then took her downstairs to the basement where he tied her with tape and shackles to the punishment pole. Then he stripped and rubbed himself over her body as she stared wide-eyed, hyperventilating, unable to understand what he was doing, or why. It wasn't until the following month that he decided to rape her. When he had finished with her, he threw her back into the bedroom where he had stashed Michelle. The two women would be kept together, both soiled, both deserving – in his opinion – of the treatment he meted out.

Michelle, who suffered the longest and the hardest, was to suffer even more as she tried to become the protector of her cell mate. She was allowed a shower only once or twice a week for the entire length of her confinement and was fed only once a day. If Castro thought, as he often did, that she was a 'bad influence' on Gina, he would lock her wrists behind her back with plastic ties – the handcuff sort used by police and security men – and drag her off to another room in the house. Often, if she whimpered when he raped her, he would stuff a filthy rag into her mouth.

The central question, at the core of the case, remains why he settled on three victims? Why not two, or ten, or thirteen? The rationale behind it holds the key to Castro's entire mad enterprise.

Dr Paul W. Ragan, the medical director of New Life Lodge, a drug and alcohol treatment centre in Burns, Tennessee, told the author of this book that the science of exploring Castro's 'sadistic personality disorder' is still in its infancy. Dr Ragan received his psychiatric training in the US navy, served with the US marines in Desert Storm, trained in addictions at the National Institutes of Health and has been an Associate Professor of Psychiatry at Vanderbilt University Medical Center for sixteen years.

He believes the perpetrator's claims of sexual abuse as a child. 'Unfortunately, there is a great taboo when talking about male-on-male sexual abuse. But child sex abuse is very, very common when dealing with people who have addictions. Intra-familial violence is far more common than people would like to acknowledge. There is about half of individuals who are sexually physically abused as children who grow up to abuse children themselves, male and female.'

But he said that Castro's dysfunctional childhood cannot be used as an excuse for his monstrous behaviour. 'There was horrendous physical abuse of Adolf Hitler by his father, who treated him like a dog. He even had a whistle he would use to call him with. His father died when he was thirteen. How these things connect to Hitler's later life are somewhat plausible, but that doesn't excuse him.

'With Castro, the number three − the number of women he kidnapped and held captive − is an interesting number psychologically, as are the roles he assigned to the women. One had his daughter, another was treated as his punching bag. What really marks this case is the degree of perversity. He loses control of his common-law wife when he lived with her in the house, and with these three women he can have total domination and control. And in a perverse way one wonders if he was trying to work through his family of origin. If someone in control wants to manipulate and exert control, three is the perfect number because he can use the triangle to play with their emotions. With two they could gang up against you, but with such a sadistic captor it is easy to show some favouritism towards two of them and ostracize the third.

'Three can also be indicative of the mom, the dad and

himself. His bad self is projected on the girl to whom he meted out the most severe punishment. The girl with whom he had the baby is the pseudo mother and the third one is assigned the qualities of either a brother or his father. He is doing to them what he had done to him. Family secrets are very corrosive to the psyche. In Castro's case, re-enactment is a prominent theme that is emerging.

'Why did he do it? What turned him into such a monster? That, of course, is the sixty-four-million-dollar question. It is not simple sociopathy. This guy is certainly not a big-time criminal, although he certainly had his issues. A psychological Einstein is needed to understand the "genetics of sadism" and put it into context with the effect on personality of an abusive childhood. Castro made a career out of it and was a pretty cool character as far as keeping it off the radar. But this is not an evil genius. He is not the smartest guy in the world. Any police officer goes to the home with a search warrant and he's in hot water.

'Neuroscience and neuropsychology are fairly stretched to try and explain this monstrosity. When you hear about cases like this and the Kampusch abduction, you wonder if it is a lot more common than anyone would think.'

The indictment meanders from rape charge to kidnapping to rape again, across the years, beginning in 2002 – when the nightmare started for Michelle – then taking in Amanda and, finally, Gina. Just the barest of details are given, which give no hint of the terror that the women underwent.

Castro raped Michelle the most frequently but then turned his attentions again to Amanda who, if Dr Ragan is correct, was the wife figure in his demonic construct. Then he went back to Michelle, and then back to Gina. They were spared only one thing: they did not have to witness the violation of each other. But they were not spared much else. On the anniversary of their kidnappings Castro baked each one a cake, with their name iced on the top, to 'celebrate' their arrival in his home. The women have told doctors that this ritual sickened them but seemed to give him much happiness. Castro, it seems, could compartmentalize his life with ease, forgetting that he had beaten, starved and abused his victims to breaking point, expecting them to share in the moments he enjoyed. They feigned happiness, of course, because to do otherwise would incur his wrath. They did not, could not, know of the conflicts that raged within their keeper.

There occurred, in 2004, a curious bout of self-reflection and self-loathing in Castro – something which was not discovered until everyone under his control had been freed. Such introspection is uncommon in abductors who revel in exerting mastery. It certainly never befell Fritzl or Priklopil, or the takers of California kidnap victim Jaycee Lee Dugard (who was an eleven-year-old schoolgirl when she was snatched off the street). True, many of them knew the difference between right and wrong, but most justified their actions by looking at themselves as superior beings who were not bound by the morals and codes of a society they despised, a society whose rules, they told themselves, were not applicable to them.

This was the one and only time Castro wavered in his mission. He took a pen and notebook and committed his innermost thoughts to a letter that ran to seven sides of paper. He tried to exonerate himself from the crimes he knew he was committing, while also claiming that his victims deserved their fate because they had got into his car, and then entered his house, without the use of force. The document is filled with self-pity.

In the letter, leaked to a local Cleveland TV reporter shortly after he was arrested, Castro talks of parental abuse as a child, culminating in being raped by an uncle, which scarred him and turned him into a 'sexual predator . . . I need help'. He also said he was contemplating suicide (although doctors at the time believed he was much too vainglorious, cowardly and self-important to exit the stage of his own making with a gesture requiring a high level of courage) and wanted to 'give all the money I saved to my victims'. He oscillated between pity and contempt for them, with contempt ultimately winning out. 'They are here against their will because they made a mistake of getting in a car with a total stranger.' But he must have known this to be totally untrue – two of the girls knew him as the father of their friend while the third, Michelle, almost certainly knew him in passing.

He also claimed that he didn't know why he kept looking for another victim, because 'I already had two in my possession'. The psychiatrists believe that this was the result of his own subconscious mind pulling him towards the magical number three – essential in order to create the family unit he thought was necessary.

Castro's letter is much briefer (and its contents not yet

fully known) than the one penned by Josef Fritzl as he stood awaiting trial in Austria. Fritzl, trying to marshal some understanding for crimes that staggered the world, wrote over 3,000 words defending himself – but suicide or guilt were never in his mind. The magical number three was also not in his plan. But a family certainly was. He wrote:

> The dream of a big family was always with me from when I was very, very small. And Rosemarie [his wife] seemed to be the perfect mother to realize that dream. This is not a good reason to marry, but it is also true to say I loved her and I still love her.

Fritzl crushed Rosemarie's soul with the rapes and the children born of incest; Castro killed his wife with his fists. Both quested after a mythical dream family, the perfect all-submissive unit that could only ever be forged out of terror and force. And just as Castro hid in plain sight, so did Fritzl. He continued in his 'explanation':

> Perhaps some people did notice what I was doing, but they really didn't care, why should they? The cellar of my house, at the end of the day, is my house, it belongs to me, it is my kingdom that only I can enter. That's what everyone knew who lived in the area. That includes my wife, my children, my tenants, and none of them ever managed to force their way into my kingdom or asked me what I did there . . . everybody obeyed my rules.

The philosophy, the mindset, of Fritzl was exactly that of Castro. And, the letter aside, Castro spent much of his time with his lawyers after his arrest trying to mitigate what he had done, trying to portray himself in as rosy a light as possible. Trying to convince a sceptical world that he was not a monster.

Dr Sherry Hamby, research professor of psychology at Sewanee, the University of the South, in Tennessee, teaches the psychology of gender and the psychology of violence, and supervises student research on violence and victimization. She is also the editor for a new journal, *Psychology of Violence*, published by the American Psychological Association, and is the author or co-author of more than seventy-five publications on family violence and youth victimization. She is fascinated by the horror of the Castro case and spoke to the author of this book.

'We watch all these movies and TV shows – and I enjoy them as much as anybody else – and we identify with these characters who, by a combination of luck and defiance of the laws of physics, can overcome tremendous odds. But the reality is that these three young women are heroes. All three of them are heroes to me. Their escape was a testament to the human spirit. The physical conditions they were confined in, and the way they were locked up – according to reports, where he could set up opportunities for them to get away and lie in wait and beat them – in reality, it was much harder for them to escape. Stockholm Syndrome is something that has been cast around but there didn't seem to be any sign of it here.

'This is easily one of the worst cases I have ever heard of. It will go down as being one of the worst on record. Although it made the case more dramatic, it probably helped the girls that there were three of them and they weren't held entirely in isolation. It may have been the case that the fact there were three of them was a huge factor in the way they were able to cope. When victims are kept alone they have no choice but to believe the propaganda of the perpetrator. I am certain there are other similar cases that haven't come to light. I don't think there is any question there are other victims in similar situations. We are only catching the dumb ones.

'I do think these girls are going to have a long recovery ahead of them. But I feel quite hopeful for the future. The evidence suggests that humans can be incredibly resilient, even after quite horrendous experiences like this. People can actually go on to become leaders in the movement against violence. The key is learning how to integrate what happened in the life story in a way that doesn't involve any denial or self-blame and also doesn't make it the only key event in their lives. That is the tricky balance.'

She said the victims can't let what happened define them. 'I think at some point it would be good to pull back from the therapeutic and turn outward to the community and other areas. Time helps with a lot of this. A lot of how they are going to handle it will depend on the kind of social support and family resources they have. These three women seem to be situated differently in terms of this. It could be more difficult for Michelle Knight who, from the reports, seems to have had problems in her life apart from this. It can be very hard to deal with situations like this for people with the very lowest socio-economic background, but mostly it depends on the strength of family and community support.

She says that people like Castro often have an extensive history of victimization themselves and suffer from 'moral disengagement', which means that they don't respond normally to people in pain. 'They experience stress and arousal differently to the rest of the population, which is why these girls had to suffer as much as they did. Look at the example of the Nazis in history. People who were leading normal lives can become murderers and get into this systemized, organized framework to carry out horrific acts over and over again. It is often a series of small steps. It doesn't happen overnight. That explains how his neighbours talked about how Castro had these social relationships and would go out in the evening to barbecues or to listen to music. That's similar to the Nazis – how they could work in the gas chambers during the day and go home to their families at night.'

If ever a template were written for Ariel Castro, his motives and the madness of his plot, then it came in the form of Jaycee Lee Dugard. Kidnapped at the age of eleven by Phillip Garrido, a methamphetamine-addicted paedophile, and his wife, she was raped from that tender age onwards until she gave birth in a squalid makeshift tent, in the backyard of his California home, in 1994.

'Phillip wanted us to be a family,' she said. 'That was his plan. I began watching videos about giving birth after I became pregnant and I worried because I knew there would be no doctor, just the kidnappers to help me. Giving birth was the most painful experience of my life. And then I saw her. She was beautiful. I felt like I wasn't alone any more. I had somebody else who was mine. I wasn't alone. And I knew then I could never let anything happen to her. I didn't know how I was going to do that, but I did.'

For the first three years, Garrido would rape her at least once a week, in terrifying sessions when he was high on methamphetamine. In later testimony to a Grand Jury – evidence which helped put her abductor and defiler behind bars for 431 years – she said, 'Phillip always said, you know, in the beginning he said that I was helping him and that, you know, he had a sex problem and that, you know, he got me so that he wouldn't have to do this to anybody else.'

She would give birth to one more daughter in captivity. 'How do you get through the things you don't want to do? You just do. I would do it all again. The most precious thing in the world came out of it . . . my daughters,' she said.

Jaycee Lee Dugard was snatched by Garrido and abducted as she walked to a school bus stop in South Lake Tahoe, California, on 10 June 1991. (Garrido had been released on parole in August 1988 after serving eleven years of a fifty-year sentence for the kidnap and rape of Katherine Callaway Hall, in 1976.) He shot her with a stun gun and pulled her into his car, then drove her to his home in Antioch where he held her captive in a concealed compound of tents and tarpaulins behind his house. As in Castro's case, the police missed two chances to save Jaycee, in November 2006 and July 2008, when Garrido was questioned by authorities regarding a neighbourhood disturbance.

She was eventually saved on 26 August 2009, when Garrido was ordered to bring his daughters to a parole meeting. Two days earlier, he had been with the girls he had fathered by his captive – then aged fifteen and eleven – to the University of California, Berkeley, looking for an event permit to distribute religious fliers. A police officer said there was 'something not right' about the children. Because Garrido was a convicted sex offender, he was told to bring the girls along to a meeting with police. Jaycee went along too, and Garrido broke down under questioning.

As her children grew up in captivity, Jaycee did her best to teach them using lesson plans she found on the internet. She was too scared to search for her mother online, as Garrido told her that he monitored her searches. In eighteen years, she didn't try to escape once. In her testimony she said she stayed, in part, because she felt she was 'helping somebody, even though it was in a really sick, perverted way. Phillip gave me this image of the world as a scary place made up of paedophiles and rapists. I have come to realize this is not true . . . One of the reasons I stayed was I wanted my kids to be safe. I was so afraid that if I tried to leave and take them with me, I wouldn't be able to protect them. I knew they were so safe in the backyard; I didn't have to worry about anyone taking them like I was taken.'

After eight years of captivity, Garrido took her outside for the first time. She had put on weight after the birth of her children, and the Garridos had dyed her hair brown, so they were convinced she wouldn't be recognized. She said she was 'so nervous when I went out, I was too paralysed by fear to ask anyone for help. I had no voice and I didn't shout to the world, "Hey, it's me, Jaycee!" even though I longed to. I could never shake the feeling that one day someone would say, "Hey, aren't you that missing girl?" But nobody ever did. I was nobody. Nobody saw me.

'For a long time in captivity I chose not to think about certain things, like my mom, because it was just too painful. I used to only allow myself to think about her on her birthday. Sometimes my mind would not cooperate. And wander with thoughts of her. Did she stay in Tahoe? Is she thinking of me?'

Nigel Horne, editor of *The Week* website, believes it was the failure of the police in both cases which extended the agony for Dugard and the Cleveland trio. He wrote:

Like the Cleveland women, Dugard might have been rescued earlier if authorities had been more assiduous. In Dugard's case, it transpired after her release that Garrido was a registered sex offender on lifetime parole for a 1976 rape case in Nevada. In 1999, the case was taken over by Californian authorities who were supposed to check on Garrido regularly.

But records show that in the course of one year – from June 2001 to July 2002 – he was never visited at all. When parole agents did visit periodically in other years they never asked to see inside Garrido's house and garden, despite commenting in their written reports that he 'acted real weird' and displayed 'real strange behaviour'.

In the Cleveland case, we now know that the police visited 2207 Seymour Avenue twice – once in response to Ariel Castro complaining about neighbours and on another occasion to ask him about an alleged incident of child abduction, after he had driven his school bus around town for two hours with a small boy in the back rather than dropping him off. If police had entered Castro's home on either of these occasions and seen the padlocked doors now described by his son, Anthony Castro, the three women might have been rescued in 2004. In short, both cases suggest a lack of care on behalf of the police and social authorities for Americans living unconventional lives in relative poverty.

As Charles Laurence reported at the time of Jaycee Dugard's rescue, the area of Antioch where Phillip Garrido hid her in a soundproofed shed in his backyard is the 'boondocks' – the sort of area people go to disappear. Seymour Avenue, Cleveland, is not the boondocks, but it is a working-class district of a city with an above-average unemployment rate of 9.5 per cent where the recession has taken its toll.

Some houses have been foreclosed for non-payment of loans and city levies – including number 2207 where, according to the Cleveland *Plain Dealer*, Ariel Castro owed $2,501 in unpaid taxes on a house valued last year at $36,100. Other houses are in a poor state because owners have little money to spend on repairs. Broken windows are sometimes simply boarded over, broken doors go unmended. There are run-down streets like Seymour Avenue in cities across America. In the most severe cases, it is hard to know whether a house is being lived in or not – and if it is, what horrors it might harbour.

Everyone in Castro's thrall suffered, both collectively and in their own way. Soon Gina was in the same virtually catatonic state of fear as Michelle, unable to scream or fight or plead with Castro for mercy when he came calling on her.

One particularly harrowing episode for all occurred between August and October 2005 – the girls cannot be more specific because the times of the day, the days of the week, were meaningless, as were the months. All they remembered was that they were all shackled and gagged and taken into the garage behind his house, where they were chained by their wrists to the handles of his van. Unable to wash or go to the lavatory, they were kept there for three terrifying days while Castro 'entertained' a visitor to his squalid house. Just who this visitor was has not been revealed.

They were, of course, grateful beyond measure when he came to release them on the fourth day.

Amanda, who had to listen to monologues from her jailer in which he tried to justify his need for her, eventually fell pregnant. Page 217 of the indictment against him says:

. . . on or about March 1 2006 to March 31 2006 defendant did engage in sexual conduct, to wit; sexual intercourse, with Jane Doe 2 by purposely compelling her to submit by force or threat of force. (Jane Doe 2's pregnancy.)

This was the nightmare she had feared ever since he began forcing himself on her. In the whispers of darkness, at times when she was lucid, Amanda was able to glean from Michelle the terrible stomach beatings she had endured to make her miscarry, with Castro's rage at fever pitch, as if she had power over her own reproductive organs. Amanda felt sure the same fate awaited her in the gloomy confines of the basement, strung up on the punishment pole.

But it was not to be.

In Castro's mind Amanda *was* the one, and her child would be living proof of their harmony, the continuity of the 'family'. He said she would have the baby. But – again, like Josef Fritzl – there would be no doctors or nurses to assist. He went to a downtown bookstore and bought a cheap book about childbirth, then stocked up on bandages, plasters and towels. He confessed in a psychiatric interview after his arrest that 'everything I knew about childbirth came from TV and involved lots of towels and someone always shouting for boiling water'. The months dragged on and, despite her condition, there was no let-up in the attacks on Amanda: he was still raping her one month from when she was due to give birth. The indictment brands him a 'sexually violent predator' – an understatement, if ever there was one.

The full story of the day of little Jocelyn's birth – 25 December 2006 – has yet to be recounted. Amanda had been his prisoner now for three years and eight months and was terrified at the prospect of giving birth in his filthy house without sterilized instruments and proper painkillers. The air was heavy with menace and the tension in the house. Gina, who had been subjected to a frenzy of rapes in the three months leading up to the birth, was told to stay in her room. Castro brought a small paddling pool into Amanda's room, one he paid $10.99 for at a sale. He figured that the afterbirth would best be contained if she had her child while sitting in it.

He ordered Michelle to be in attendance, and issued a grave threat to her: 'The baby dies, you do too, bitch.'

She knew it was not an idle threat – she bore the injuries of his wrath to prove it. She was silent as Amanda lowered herself into the paddling pool, wondering what made her so special that she was allowed to give life when all he had ever done was take her babies away from her. A carer for Michelle has revealed to the author that Castro revelled in the 'potency' of his new role as creator, life-giver, fertile seed-god. He may have made only a few hundred bucks a week, but he was omnipotent here, in his kingdom. As Amanda went into labour her breathing became heavy and she screamed out in pain. Castro turned the sound up on his hi-fi system, masking her screams with the notes of a jaunty merengue number. There was no epidural or any strong painkillers. Amanda had to make do with a packet of Advil – headache tablets – which Castro had bought from a local gas station. She gripped Michelle's hands tightly. Michelle, who had given birth to Joey. Michelle, who had lost him. Michelle, who knew what to do.

Suddenly, after what seemed like hours of labour, there was a last push from an exhausted Amanda and a wrinkled baby, no bigger than a shoebox, was suddenly lying there on the plastic. The only problem was that the infant was not making any noise.

Michelle looked at Castro. Amanda's eyes were closed with exhaustion. The eyes of the jailer narrowed into slits. Michelle may have been bullied at school for being slow, but there was nothing slow in her reactions this day. She knew that her own life depended on what happened in the next few seconds, as well as that of the child.

'She scooped up the baby,' said the carer, later, 'and she began giving it mouth-to-mouth. Michelle was no trained paramedic but she had enough gut instinct to know she had to get that little mite's collapsed lungs parted and operating.'

One, two, three . . . pause . . . breathe . . . one, two, three . . .

The baby seemed to be turning blue, its wrinkled skin cold against her touch. But then there was a cough, a trickle of phlegm and, finally, a full-throated cry.

Merry Christmas, Jocelyn, Amanda, Michelle and Gina.

A miracle of life had occurred in Seymour Avenue which spared them all for another day.

Castro created the baby, and he named it. He opted for Jocelyn because he is a great fan of Jocelyn Lorette Brown, sometimes credited as Jocelyn Shaw, an American R&B and dance music singer. He loved the baby too – he really did – and never harmed her. He bought the child fluffy romper suits, little dolls, soft toys in stores far away from his home, and purchased baby formula to feed her. Castro had cemented another brick into the edifice he was intent on building, although the family – *his* family – would remain a secret from the outside world.

The assaults on all three women continued, and he continued to forbid them from having contact with each other as a trio. Michelle could be with Amanda, Amanda could be with Gina, Michelle could be with Gina, but he feared all three in a conclave against him. Such was their mental state that, by and large, they abided by his rules. Sometimes he even allowed them to cook for him on the rare occasions he brought home fresh groceries. But they were never out of his sight when at the stove.

The doors to the rooms upstairs were sometimes left unlocked, but all the women had suffered from his 'testing' – when he pretended to leave but actually lay in wait for them – and, as a result, were programmed to do as he said whenever he actually did step beyond the front door. They all remained quiet – or as quiet as they could, given that a baby accepts no commands when it is hungry, tired or fractious – whenever he brought people around. Often, they would hear the voices above the music from downstairs. They would have heard policemen knocking on the door on the two occasions when officers came to see him. But they could do nothing. They had lapsed into states of total passivity which, in the cases of Gina and Michelle, were interrupted by thoughts of self-harm and even suicide.

And yet, the women strove for normality in the midst of such hideous circumstances. Keeping secret diaries was one way of exercising their minds. Years later, the prosecutor who would bring Castro to justice said, 'They were able to mark the passage of time through the maintenance of diaries. Several diary entries document abuse and life as a captive. The entries speak of forced sexual conduct, of being locked in a dark room, of anticipating the next session of abuse, of the dreams of some day escaping and being reunited with family, of being chained to a wall, of being held like a prisoner of war, of missing the lives they once enjoyed, of emotional abuse, of his threats to kill, of being treated like an animal, of continuous abuse, and of desiring freedom.'

They clung to the hope of freedom like a shipwrecked survivor clasping a broken piece of wood amid the waves. Amanda, of course, now had something to live for. In this, her experience parallels that of Elisabeth Fritzl.

The first child Elisabeth gave birth to in the cellar, daughter Kerstin, was like a booster shot to the soul, giving her a reason for living that was beyond the depraved fantasies of her father. When, aged forty-two, she emerged blinking into the world of light that she had left behind when she was eighteen, the experts said it was her maternal instincts which had kept her sane, kept her mind vigorous. 'She was a true heroine,' said Wolfgang Bergmann, head of the Institute for Child Psychology in the German city of Hanover. 'She survived through, and for, her offspring. The strength of a mother's love is best illustrated in extremis.'

As for Elisabeth, so with Amanda. She adored her baby, begged Castro to buy books for her to read to little Jocelyn, taught her the nursery rhymes her own mother had sung to her as a baby. She made promises to her daughter that, whatever happened, whatever more she had to endure, one day, one day all this would end. She would be free.

Until that day, life with a baby and its attendant health and hygiene problems made the house a pretty unpleasant place in which to live. There were the smells of unwashed bodies, old food, grime, bedclothes that needed washing, towels that needed changing, nappies – no wonder the jailer was keen to leave his captives to their own devices and seek down time through the relatively relaxing pursuit of playing music to an appreciative audience.

'He has indicated,' said an investigator, later, 'that he began to feel high levels of stress after the birth of Jocelyn because he had no endgame in sight to his strategy. He wanted a family – check. He wanted a child with a "suitable" mother – check. He wanted sex on demand – check. He wanted secrecy check. But he ran out of tick boxes in his head because, in truth, his plan was conceived on the hoof and made up as he went along. He liked the Jekyll and Hyde persona before the birth of Jocelyn but it required another level of subterfuge with her around. He knew he had to take her out, let her get sunlight and fresh air. That is when he coached her to remain silent about the "other ladies", both of whom were not permitted to reveal their real names to her for fear that, one day, she might inadvertently slip up when he was introducing her as his granddaughter or, as was more common, the daughter of a woman-friend of his.'

Neighbour Juan Perez recalled, 'I remember her well enough, and plenty of people saw her. She was a pretty little thing. He was real attentive towards her. I remember asking him on the street whose kid she was, and he just said "a friend's". Hard to imagine the kind of things he must have told her, to keep her playing his game, isn't it? I mean, the kid could have sunk him at any time if she told someone on the street that she lived in a house with three ladies, some of whom were chained up!'

Castro believed the baby was his: his to indulge, his to spoil, his to show off, his to indoctrinate. But like the bond between Elisabeth Fritzl and her cellar tribe, and between Jaycee Lee Dugard and her daughters, the bond between Amanda and her daughter was stronger than he could ever have imagined. And in denying it, Castro had made the biggest mistake of his life. It was not to him that little Jocelyn turned for affection, but to her mother. It was not to him that she turned for knowledge, but to her patient mother who, amidst the squalor, taught her to count and read and told her about the wonderment of life. When Jocelyn questioned her about why she and the 'other ladies' could not go out, Amanda told her fantastical stories, pledging that, 'One day, it will all be different.'

That day came, in May 2013. Mommy kept her word.

It was Jocelyn who would now send Castro to hell.

5. Immaculate Deception

One thousand and ninety-nine times.

That is on how many occasions the Cleveland Police Department showed up on Seymour Avenue during the time that Ariel Castro had his 'family' in captivity. They came to break up fights, to cool marital rows, to chase sexual exhibitionists, suspected burglars, vandals, drunks and deadbeats. On one occasion, twenty people were slugging it out in the middle of the road with baseball bats, their shouting and screaming surely heard by the denizens of the unknown jailhouse. The fact that Castro's house was one of the quietest on the block went to the heart of his master plan: hide in plain sight, keep your nose clean, keep the women quiet and cowed. He managed all three – and his day job, to boot.

On average, police cruisers rolled into Seymour Avenue once every three and a half days, from August 2002 (the vanishing of Michelle Knight) until the day of the escapes. The women were separated from them by wooden walls stuffed with insulating foam and the crudely blacked-out windows. But they might as well have been on the other side of the Atlantic Ocean. Departmental police records released in the first days after the breakout showed how, in the words of the criminal behavioural expert, the 'social and economic decay' of Seymour Avenue aided and abetted Castro's master plan.

The NBC broadcasting company, which obtained the police call-out logs together with follow-up reports, noted:

> The records offer a clue to a central mystery of the case: How could the women have gone undiscovered for so long? Castro's whitewashed home – despite its covered windows and padlocked front door – was one of the quietest on a chaotic block, one of the houses making the fewest reports to police. The neighborhood emerges from the police records as a central character in the crime story, a declining neighborhood in social turmoil. Why would the quiet house on the block draw a second glance from officers who are responding to domestic abuse calls and flashers, to broken windows and prowlers, to a fight involving twenty people armed with baseball bats?

Khalid Samad, the community organizer at the forefront of the hunt for the missing women down the years, told of an incident that occurred just after the joyous scenes of freedom. 'Not an hour after they're out, I'm standing on the street near the Castro house and a fight broke out a few doors down because a guy who was out there saw a guy who he recognized as having shot him on the street. Dude took off running, and they're wrestling down in front of the church.'

He went on to describe this incident as characteristic of the chaos at the heart of Seymour Avenue. 'That's the kind of thing that would go on there. I believe the women might not have gone unnoticed in a different neighbourhood. If this was an inner-ring suburban neighbourhood you'd have some nosy neighbours who would ask, "Why are your windows boarded up? Why are you taking groceries in, if you don't have family there?" Around here, no one asked those questions. They kept out of things.'

The logs show police activity virtually everywhere – except at the door of 2207.

At number 2115 police visited thirty-seven times, at 2120 – across the street and a little way along – they knocked on the door sixty-eight times. And right next door to chez Castro, they were called out thirty-five times.

Juan Perez, a man who works with autism sufferers, lived just a few doors down from Castro. He told the author of this book, 'That's the thing about this street – what would be crazy anywhere else is taken as normal. Ariel knew that. That's why, like, when he went out with the little girl, he would introduce her to people he met either as his granddaughter or the daughter of a girlfriend. But no one thought to say, hey, wait a minute: we ain't never seen Ariel with no girlfriend. He just calculated on people not asking too many questions, I guess. Long as he could keep the police from his stoop, I figure he figured he was cool.'

The day after Gina disappeared, police were at 2022 Seymour, investigating threatening telephone calls, while the records show that on 6 April 2007 police were almost outside Castro's front door when two cars were involved in an accident. Police were in attendance for nearly an hour and a half. The crazy baseball-bat melee took place over the 4th July holiday weekend in 2006, and five police cars were dispatched, but officers knocked at Castro's door only twice during the 3,910 days and nights that Michelle, the longest of the captives, was missing. Neither call had anything to do with the missing females.

Call number one came on 26 January 2004 and was in connection with the boy left on board Castro's school bus while he went for lunch at a Wendy's fast-food restaurant. The second visit came about when Castro himself called the police regarding a fight in his street.

According to NBC, some of the call-outs to Seymour Avenue during the time he was there concerned 'women screaming', but it was never established where the noises came from. One of those was on 20 January 2003 when a woman with poor eyesight at 2115 Seymour Avenue – just a few doors down from Castro's house – rang to say she could hear 'a woman screaming out front'. A police officer arrived five minutes later and stayed for forty-five minutes. Nothing more was heard, so he drove off. She called again on 6 May 2008, claiming to have heard a woman shouting, 'Get off me!' She also claimed to have heard a baby crying. A police officer arrived, stayed on the scene for nineteen minutes and then left, none the wiser.

Israel Lugo, who lives two homes down from Castro, said he heard pounding on some of the doors of Castro's house, which had plastic bags on the windows, in November 2011. In that case police responded to his call, but officers only knocked on the front door and left when no one answered. 'They walked to the side of the house and then left,' Lugo said.

The police records contain no mention of ever being called out by neighbours who claimed, after the rescue, to have seen the inmates of the Castro house once being led around naked and chained in the backyard like dogs. The captives themselves have since denied these reports.

'There is no evidence to indicate that any of them were ever outside in the yard, in chains, without clothing, or any other manner,' said Martin Flask, Cleveland Director of Public Safety.

Police Chief Michael McGrath added, 'We have no record of anyone calling to report anything suspicious about the Castro house.'

Privately, officers were seething about the recovered-memory tales of these 'armchair detectives' and believe some were made in bad faith in an attempt to embarrass the force, for whatever reason.

'I can tell you personally that I busted my butt to find those girls,' said Keith Sulzer, Cleveland Police District Commander, at a community meeting on 9 May. 'Me and my guys searched every vacant lot, every vacant building, everywhere that we could legally go in and search.'

'The fact was,' said Deputy Police Chief Edward Tomba, 'no one went to the house without being invited. Castro was extraordinarily protective of his home. Even his brothers had no idea about Castro's imprisoned victims. You didn't get into his house. You called before you went over. He ran the show and he acted alone.'

Seven houses – some of them unoccupied – flank Castro's house, and nine houses and two apartment buildings are on the other side. The boarded-up buildings do not look dissimilar to Castro's; there was nothing that called out to the casual passer-by that evil deeds lurked within. Yet the general aura of neglect, of dilapidation, belies, say the residents, a feeling of solidarity among those who live there.

Rick Shear, a retired tow-truck driver, told the author, 'It is not just a neighbourhood, it's a community. We all have everyone's backs, we watch people's houses and vehicles. We cook out and have barbecues. I even went to a backyard barbecue at Ariel's place, although I never went inside. Looking back, I guess it was a little suspicious that he kept his blinds constantly lowered and had this stuff over his windows, but it really isn't that unusual for people to want their privacy. Many residents along Seymour Avenue keep to themselves.'

Ellie Johnson, aged eighty-one, who has lived in the neighbourhood since 1992, concurred, saying he remembered a time when 'children played outside and firework shows lighted the skies. That stopped several years ago as families grew older and people became more isolated. It's a bit rough, but I love it here. People treat me nice and others don't bother me.'

Dr Matt Logan, a former veteran of the Royal Canadian Mounted Police for twenty-eight years, left the service to pursue a new career as a provider of forensic behavioural consultations and training for law enforcement and criminal justice officials. He has advised numerous forces on serious crime issues, child exploitation, psychological risk and threat assessments. He is also a trained FBI hostage negotiator.

He said, 'There's a tendency to think that an individual would have to be fairly sophisticated in order to keep up appearances while holding another person captive for years on end. But the more I look at this case, I'm guessing that it's actually going against that. I think Castro was just very lucky in what he'd done. His victims suffered, but he pulled it off with a combination of cunning and luck, perhaps because of the neighbourhood in which he lived.'

While the police defended their record in the call-out cases – saying that the logs were proof of their vigilance, their responsiveness – feelings emerged that things might have been different if only everything was not about money. *Slate* website reporter Justin Peter seemed to hit the nail on the head for many in an article beneath a headline that read: 'Did the Cleveland Cops Botch the Search for the Missing Women?' He wrote:

> Cops can't enter a house without permission or a warrant, and they can't get a warrant without probable cause. Ariel Castro did not have a long criminal record, and there was no reason to suspect that anything was actually happening there. I've seen it implied that Castro's record of domestic abuse and his poor performance as a school bus driver should have triggered suspicions. These things may well have triggered suspicions that Ariel Castro was a jerk. It's unreasonable to expect, though, that the cops could have magically inferred that he was holding three women captive in his house.

In a recent column in *The Plain Dealer*, Mark Naymik wrote that the disappearances of DeJesus and Berry, at least, were a long-time departmental priority:

I've seen police follow up on the most tenuous of leads, from teenagers too young to remember DeJesus' disappearance.

Other reports bear this out (for example, as already stated, the cops dug up a vacant lot in 2012 after a convict falsely informed them that Berry's body could be found there). But Naymik makes another important point that hasn't been cited elsewhere:

At the moment, the hum of criticism on Seymour Avenue is about the subtle signs, such as the lowered shades or odd behavior of Castro and how he never entertained guests. These are the kinds of signs that police officers who patrol a specific beat over time might notice or hear about from neighbors. But that kind of patrol disappeared when community policing ended.

'That kind of patrol disappeared when community policing ended' – that's the line you should remember if you're looking to criticize the cops here. Intuition is one of a police officer's foremost assets. But missing persons and odd behavior become suspicious only when you are intimately familiar with a neighborhood, with what normalcy means, and when normalcy is breached. In Cleveland and elsewhere, that sort of hyper-local knowledge is on the wane. Despite a high crime rate, the city, facing budget shortfalls, has laid off police officers and downsized the department over the past decade. As the president of the Cleveland Police Patrolmen's Association wrote in a letter to *The Plain Dealer* in 2010: 'The Cleveland Police Department has never recovered from the 2004 downsizing of 252 police officers. We have been working with no Auto Theft, Community Policing or Gang units.'

All of the criticisms over police behavior in this case are actually criticisms of the do-more-with-less modern policing mentality, of the disappearance of the beat cop in favor of specialized units that are ostensibly more effective and efficient. And they might be more effective and efficient when it comes to dropping a city's crime rate over the short term. But the fact that Michelle Knight, Amanda Berry and Gina DeJesus spent years in a house in a dense Cleveland neighborhood is one indication of the long-term problems with this approach. In the end, the Cleveland police and its critics are both right. The cops likely did all they could to sniff out where the missing women were being held. But in this age of departmental budget cuts, all they could do wasn't nearly enough.

It is beyond galling for the families of the missing women to think that their ordeals were prolonged simply for the sake of dollar bills. America spent close to $800 *billion* on its foreign defence budget in 2004. That same year, Cleveland laid off 250 police officers – 15 per cent of its total force – in drastic budget cuts following news there was a $60 million hole in city finances. Detectives were assigned to patrol duties; specialized units such as the gang and auto-theft squads were eliminated; mini-stations spread around poor neighbourhoods were closed and the community police officers who worked there were returned to patrol cars.

America could find the money to pursue foreign wars in Afghanistan and Iraq but not, it seems, to take the fight to criminals in the heart of many of its broken-down cities.

Down all the years that the searches and vigils and prayer meetings went on for the missing women, Castro kept up his charade of being the kindly guy on the block, befriended by all. It suited his purposes admirably for police to be drawn over a thousand times to other distractions in the neighbourhood, because it kept all eyes off him – especially when it came to feeding and clothing his inmates.

Like Josef Fritzl, who travelled miles from his home-town in Amstetten, Austria, to buy sanitary supplies and food – and, eventually, the medical equipment necessary for his daughter to give birth in the darkness to his children – Castro ventured far and wide for the necessities to keep his 'family' alive. Like Fritzl, he was a committed cheapskate. He cut vouchers from newspapers to redeem special offers at supermarkets. He bought the women sanitary items at the Dollar family supermarket near Cleveland's historic covered market and ventured as far away as twenty miles to buy groceries. He stuffed his fridge with soft drinks on special offer and mostly fed the women either on frozen pizzas or on fast food from a variety of outlets – McDonald's, Wendy's, Kentucky Fried Chicken.

William Perez, the proprietor of Belinda's nightclub where Castro performed so often, was later to remember the finger food he laid out for customers on weekends. Smiling as if he could kick himself, he said, 'You know, when the news broke about what he did, I suddenly remembered something really weird about the guy. At weekends we would have all this bar food – you know, chicken wings, empanadas, bits of pork, enchiladas, dips, tacos, all sorts of stuff. And often Ariel would come up to me after a gig and say, "Can I buy some of this stuff?" And he would, you know, be walking off with twenty to thirty dollars' worth of food, bags stuffed full of food. It never occurred to me to ask why, even though we knew he was a loner and we knew he lived alone. We never put it together, never joined up the dots. Son of a bitch! Of course, *now* we know why he needed all that food! I hope those women enjoyed it, is all.'

Neighbours, too, saw Castro lumbering into the house with brown bags from fast-food restaurants, clearly bulging with more than enough for one, or even two, people to eat. Then there were the occasions when they saw him struggling to unload tinned meat and soups from his car – so much stuff, in fact, that some neighbours thought he might be a survivalist, one of the fruit cakes who believed that the end was nigh, and he was preparing to hunker down inside while society plunged into disaster.

Javier Marti, living almost directly opposite, said, 'I often wondered what a single guy needed with so much stuff. I mean, his brothers came over and all, and sometimes his musician friends, but it's not like he was the kind of guy to hold a dinner party. He was much more the sling-it-on-the-barbecue kind of man. And yet I would say to my mom, "What's he *doing* with all that food?" But what you gonna do? Call the cops because your neighbour has a food fixation?'

And a fixation it seemed to be. As well as his excursions to distant discount supermarkets, he also frequented church-hall food banks where comestibles were on offer for society's poor to help themselves, or to purchase at a knock-down price. Clearly, Castro struggled to feed four people – five, after Jocelyn came along – on his meagre bus driver's salary. He had to take what he could get, where he could get it. Even though he often told his brothers, Onil and Pedro, that he was committed to a healthy lifestyle – he boasted about growing greens on a vegetable patch so he could stay 'in good shape' – he was, in fact, a slave to everything fast, calorific and fattening. Which meant, of course, that his 'family' had to be too. He illegally traded in food stamps – the US welfare handouts to those on the breadline – paying people less than their face value so they could buy cigarettes and liquor, which were unredeemable on the stamps, and he could then obtain more cut-price food for his victims. It is estimated that almost half the houses in his neighbourhood receive food stamps, so they were a commodity that was easy to obtain and easy to trade.

While stocking his house with food to keep everyone alive, Castro operated another form of deception to keep attention away from himself: he attended the rallies and the prayer meetings for the missing girls, to give the impression that he was as horrified as everyone else about their disappearance. He would sing along with other parishioners at the Immanuel Evangelical Lutheran Church, at the corner of his street, and bow his head in a display of grotesque piety as the Reverend Horst Hoyer beseeched his flock 'to keep their faith in God and pray for the safe return of these poor women'. Amen, Castro would mouth in unison with the others.

In 2004 he was to receive an unlikely ally in his faux concern – his own son, Anthony. Father and son had a difficult relationship, due to the beatings he administered to both Anthony and his mother, Grimilda, when the boy was growing up. But contact was maintained, and the pair had conversations at the house about the missing girls, Amanda and Gina.

Anthony had no way of knowing that the girls were a few feet above his head. He, too, was told never to venture either upstairs or downstairs in the house he had once called home. Indeed, in a house that was chock full of painful memories, he had no desire to do so. Anthony, whose first name was the same as his father's but who mostly went by his middle name, interviewed Gina's mother in 2004 for a story he wanted to write while a journalism student at Bowling Green State University. It was published in the *Plain Press* in June 2004.

Managing editor Chuck Hoven said that Anthony – a student looking to expand his writing portfolio – volunteered to do the story for free. 'He did a good job. At the time, it was a big story for us and he was from the neighbourhood.'

This was what he wrote – unaware, like the rest of society, that his father would have made a much better interview subject.

How Gina DeJesus' disappearance has
changed her neighborhood
by Ariel [Anthony] Castro

Since April 2, 2004, the day 14-year-old Gina DeJesus was
last seen on her way home from Wilbur Wright Middle
School, neighborhood residents have been taken by an
overwhelming need for caution. Parents are more strictly
enforcing curfews, encouraging their children to walk in
groups, or driving them to and from school when they
had previously walked alone.

'You can tell the difference,' DeJesus' mother, Nancy
Ruiz, said. 'People are watching out for each other's kids.
It's a shame that a tragedy had to happen for me to really
know my neighbors. Bless their hearts, they've been
great.'

On Cleveland's west side, it is difficult to go any length
of time without seeing Gina's picture on telephone poles,
in windows, or on cars along the busy streets.

'People are really looking out for my daughter,' Ruiz said.

For seven weeks, Gina's family has been organizing
searches, holding prayer vigils, posting fliers and calling
press conferences. Despite the many tips and rumors that
have been circulating in the neighborhood, there has been
no sign of her.

One thing is for certain, however. Almost everyone
feels a connection with the family, and Gina's disappearance has the whole area talking.

'It's traumatized a lot of people,' Bob Zak, Safety
Coordinator of the Westown Community Development

Corporation, said. 'People are suspicious of everyone. Kids, parents, and grandparents are afraid.'

The organization serves Cleveland's Ward 19, which stretches from West Boulevard to West 134th Street.

Parents and relatives waiting for their children as school let out at Wilbur Wright recently expressed concern about the number of sex offenders living and working in the area.

'I really believe there needs to be more security,' Vaneetha Smith said as she waited for her niece outside Wilbur Wright Middle School at the end of the day. 'We have too many kidnappings, and they should crack down on all the sex offenders in the area.'

Luis Perez echoed Smith's concerns as he waited for his niece at the school.

'I think the neighborhood is pretty bad,' he said. 'You have to be aware of some people out there.'

The Ohio Electronic Sex Offender Registration and Notification (eSORN) database lists 133 sex offenders living or working in Gina's immediate zip code. Many residents of the area, however, cannot use the database, as they do not have access to the Internet at home.

'I have been here almost four years and I have been notified of only one sex offender,' Ruiz said. 'And he lives only about 1,000 feet away from here.'

Ohio law prohibits sex offenders who are required to register from establishing their residence within 1,000 feet of school buildings.

'There is no enforcing the laws because they still live right next to the schools and the bus stops,' Ruiz said.

She believes the process of registering sex offenders is essentially a waste of time.

At a Ward 19 crime watch meeting, one of ten monthly, residents describe the area as a multi-ethnic community where people work and try to keep their housing up to par. They feel the disappearance of Amanda Berry on April 21, 2003 was a wake-up call, but Gina's case really caught everyone's attention.

Many residents believe the schools and the city have more work to do to help out.

'There is not enough supervision at the schools and when the kids get out, they still run through the streets,' Smith said. 'They say that once they leave the school premises, the school is not responsible for them. But until they reach their house, I believe they are. They should be more concerned with their safety.'

'The school is supposed to be a safe place,' Perez said. 'They need more police around the schools, surrounding the area. Without that, it's just going to keep on going and there will be more innocent people getting hurt.'

Isaac Rodriguez has seen some changes happen at Wilbur Wright.

'There are more security guards at the school now,' the father of two middle school students said. 'They have been having assemblies and talking to the kids about the danger.'

'When you send your kids out to school now,' Smith said, 'you don't know if they are going to make it home or not. From West 105th to [West 110th], anything could happen. I feel the mayor should do something about that. The children should be our first priority, no matter what else is going on in the city.'

Zak, a former Cleveland police officer of 30 years, believes the community is feeling the effects of the city's cuts in the police force.

'The first thing a city should do is protect its citizens,' he said. Although police cannot be on the scene of every crime as they occur, Zak reports that residents are getting responses to calls 'one, two, and four hours later.'

Cuts in the police force are not the only budget changes that are directly affecting residents. The Cleveland Municipal School District is also mulling over how it will eliminate its projected $100 million budget deficit. Among the items cut will be purchased services, employee overtime, supplemental pay, textbooks, school staff and student transportation.

It pains Anthony Castro now to think that his father took the friend of his own daughter as one of his sex slaves. He now wants nothing to do with him.

Dr Anthony Nuccitelli, New York State licensed psychologist, certified forensic consultant and founder of iPredator Inc., says Castro's behaviour during the women's long incarceration showed both his organizational skills and 'talents for deception'. In an interview for this book he explained Castro's mindset.

'He appears to be a classic sociopath with no remorse, shame or guilt. He viewed women throughout life as targets, opportunities and objects. And his ability to pathologically lie, manipulate and con displayed a high level of criminal versatility. Before they set foot in that house he would have fantasized about exercising control over every aspect of their lives and would have made them, in return, show respect, gratitude and love, or what he thought were such things. He would have oscillated between rage and abuse, switching to small expressions of love and approval when interacting with the victims, creating an addictive cycle between himself and the targeted victim. But at all times, in public arenas, he would turn on a superficial charm and present himself as conventional and "normal".

'I classify him as a malignant sociopath, a disturbed person who exhibits the extreme form of sociopathy, does not suffer from an acute psychiatric mental illness, is predominantly driven by the need for absolute power and control, and views the enslavement of their victims as a priority – as opposed to taking their life – engaging in sexual and/or violent victimization, stealing their valuables or causing them psychological distress.

'This case includes extreme deviance. It is not madness, it is not close to madness. For those who study this criminal case, it is absolutely incredible. What it comes down to is ten years. In and of itself, that is just incredible. These women surrendered to the fight inside that house, not because they wanted to, but because they had to. And once on the outside he was able to walk through life presenting himself just as a regular joe. You would never know, not in a million years, that the person you were talking to really has three people back home chained up in his basement.

'Unfortunately, we walk through life and we hear these stories and tend to think of a monster, an ogre, incredibly ugly, and he would be walking down the road a half a mile ahead and you would sense he was evil incarnate. No. The only solution is to teach your children not to walk through life with paranoia, but at least a small amount of caution.

'I think the mannequin that he drove around the city with in his car is a key to his personality. It reminds me a little of the character of Norman Bates in Hitchcock's *Psycho* where amateur taxidermist Bates has preserved the body of his late mother and keeps it in a rocking chair in her bedroom. The stuffed mother was a touchstone for Bates in the way that this mannequin was for Castro. I would love to learn more about it, but I guess that the mannequin fulfilled a role for him before he was able to carry out his plan to steal real people and keep them under control. It was a significant totem for him.

'He must have been operating at terrific pressure in that house. He has to work, he has to provide for them, he has to keep them secret. And he has to keep his mask of normalcy on at all times when he is outside. The smallest slip-up would cost him everything, and he knew this, all the time. It was a fantastic charade to pull off. He was no crazy guy, just a cunning one, able to handle this incredible pressure all the time.'

External pressures may have weighed heavily on him, but the daily routine was the same for Castro. He got up most days at 6.00 a.m. and took cereal and coffee to the 'family'. He was out of the house by 7.00 a.m. and at the wheel of the bus by 8.00 a.m. He worked until around midday, usually lunched at a fast-food outlet but some-times took food home for the captives. He would then work again until around 5.00 p.m. on the school run. If he was playing in a band gig, he would return home to check on everyone, freshen up and make sure the house was secure before he left. If he was in for the evening, he would fantasize about which female would be allowed to 'pleasure' him that evening.

The only thing Ariel Castro always made sure of was that the locks were securely in place. He slept on the same floor as the captive family, ensuring their silence and their compliance during the hours of darkness.

In 2007, the pressure got worse for Castro. It was his other family – the one he had raised with Grimilda – who began to trouble him. His beloved daughter Emily was jailed for twenty-five years, for trying to murder her own child. Emily had by then moved to Fort Wayne with her mother, Grimilda.

Emily slashed her daughter Janyla's throat four times with a knife on 4 April 2007, the day after the baby's father moved out of their home. The baby was eleven months old at the time and was rushed out of the apartment, into the street, by Grimilda who was screaming for help. As medics attended to the child, police found Emily a few blocks away covered in mud, water and blood. Emily, who was nineteen at the time of the attack on the baby, had a self-inflicted knife wound to her neck and wrists and tried to drown herself in a nearby creek, according to the court.

She tried to claim insanity at her trial but this was

rejected by prosecutors who found her competent to stand trial, albeit recognizing that she suffered from a 'mental illness'. She was sentenced on 17 January 2008.

Court records show Emily was diagnosed with manic depression when she was just thirteen years old, almost certainly brought on by witnessing the violence against her mother. This spiralled into delusions that her own family were out to kill her and her baby. She had a history of stopping and refusing medications and treatments for her mental illness. She argued in an appeal against her sentence, in November of 2008, that this had not been taken into account at her original trial. Emily told the judge that she was a good mother and she did not know how it could have happened.

Her brother, Anthony, read out a statement in court in defence of his sister and her mental illness, which said:

What happened to Janyla was serious, unthinkable and irreversible. What happened to my sister is no less serious. Emily's mental illness was something the family saw every day, and it was regrettable it failed to meet the legal definition of insanity. She was not an animal who tried to kill her daughter out of revenge but a proud mother who put together scrapbooks in anticipation of Janyla's first birthday.

Emily lost the appeal and Janyla was given over for custody to Deangelo Gonzalez.

Castro was devoted to his daughter. Any normal father would have made the journey to Fort Wayne to stand up for his offspring. But Castro was not normal and could not leave the house unattended. Austrian captor Josef Fritzl had built an elaborate dungeon for his rape object, his own daughter, complete with sealed doors and freezers stuffed full of cheap food. He would take himself off for up to three weeks at a time for holidays in Thailand, where he indulged himself with prostitutes and enjoyed plentiful amounts of cheap drink. He knew there would be no escape for his captive or the incest children.

Castro was cunning but no genius. His prison was a cheap house made of wood that he had to guard like a hawk in order to preserve its secrets. The nearest thing he had to security, beyond the window coverings and the locks on the doors, was a truck wing mirror that he mounted on to a back wall of the garage, in his yard, which he could see from the kitchen. It would reflect back immediately anyone trying to enter the yard. Castro never took a vacation and was never away for longer than a working day or an evening spent playing bass at the local guitar clubs.

An investigator on the case later said, 'After he was arrested he expressed remorse for many things, one of them being that he was not able to travel to the trial of Emily to stand up for her. He regrets what happened to her and blames himself for the way she was brought up. He knows he did wrong, but he is a psychopath, and one of those traits is doing the same thing over and over again, always hoping for a different result. It was like that with Grimilda. He knew he was wrong to beat her but he couldn't stop doing it.

'I think that he really was trying to build the family he never had in this house of his, but his controlling, evil personality meant it was warped. It didn't stop him having human feelings from time to time, especially for his daughter, but struggling to keep his secret world going meant he could not venture out into the real one for extended periods. And that meant not being able to support his own flesh and blood.'

Thursday 12 June 2008. 8.35 p.m. Perhaps the greatest single chance to derail Castro's scheme was squandered when a Cleveland police officer with 10,000 arrests under his belt allowed Castro to go free after he was pulled over on his motorcycle and found to be in violation of several laws.

Officer Jim Simone, a video camera mounted in his patrol vehicle, sees a bike go flying by him with the rear number plate tilted to one side. This is an old trick, often used by illegal riders who don't want the registration number to be easily identifiable. Castro, wearing a white vest and shorts, pulls ahead of Officer Simone – a father of three daughters – into a Shell filling station, the dashboard camera of the police car picking up everything. Officer Simone follows him on to the forecourt. Castro, with three women and a child in his house, looks nervous on the videotape as the policeman approaches.

OFFICER SIMONE: Let me see your driver's licence.
CASTRO: Excuse me?

OFFICER SIMONE: Let me see your driver's licence, please.

CASTRO: What's wrong?

OFFICER SIMONE: First off, your plate's improperly displayed, it has to be displayed left to right, not upside down or sideways.

[*Castro mumbles something.*]

OFFICER SIMONE: The law says you have to be able to read it from behind.

CASTRO: I just got it out so –

OFFICER SIMONE: Where's your motorcycle endorsement? The office asked.

CASTRO: That I don't have.

OFFICER SIMONE: Another question is why you riding it then? You don't have a helmet on, you don't have a licence to operate it – you're setting yourself to be arrested. Is that what you want?

CASTRO: No, sir, I don't want that.

OFFICER SIMONE: The law says you have to be able to read 'em from behind.

[*Castro again mumbles something about this being the first time he has taken the bike out and fails to produce a licence to ride it.*]

OFFICER SIMONE: These plates don't belong to this bike, do they? What year Yamaha is this?

CASTRO: This is 2000.

OFFICER SIMONE: Where's the Harley if the plates are gone?

CASTRO: Oh, the Harley. I sold it and I traded it in for this one.

OFFICER SIMONE: Well, Ariel, you keep getting deeper and deeper and deeper.

CASTRO: I know, but I just got off work. I'm a school bus driver. And . . .

In the end, Officer Simone, now retired, said he had a choice to make – take Castro downtown and book him, or let him off with a warning and write him two tickets on the spot. Castro displayed all the behaviour that psychiatric experts say allowed him to fool the world for so long – politeness, deference to authority, a humbling attitude. Any hint of aggression or backchat to the police officer would have seen him run in. As it was, Officer Simone said he actually felt sorry for him, that in booking him he might be consigning him to life on welfare. Afterwards, when criticism of his actions was aired on TV and in newspapers, Officer Simone defended himself.

'Well, actually, he was arrestable. He didn't have a licence to operate a motorcycle and normally I would arrest people for that, but he was very polite and he explained to me he was a school bus driver, so if I had physically arrested him and towed his bike there was a good possibility he might have lost his job as a school bus driver, so I took that into consideration and I made him – I gave him a couple of tickets – I made him push the bike all the way home. After the story broke about the girls and everything, I reflected on this many times. And actually, if I had arrested him, I would have cuffed him, put him in the car, towed his motorcycle away and took him to jail. But there'd have been no reason to go to his house. And in addition, these girls were chained inside. It's a good thing that I let him go, actually. At least I know that they got fed and weren't alone locked up in that house without him. Especially since there was a small baby involved.

'What happened, I was at dinner and it was on TV. It came on the news, everybody in the restaurant stood up, applauded, started hugging each other. And then they came out, they were all alive. So it was a great day for me. I know it was a great day for them and a great day for the Cleveland Police Department. But it didn't ring any bells until the media contacted me. And I have at my house about three thousand videos. I videotaped the last eighteen years of my career. And when they called me, they knew I would have the video, they knew I would have a copy of the ticket. So I went home, I researched it, I found the copy of the ticket on the stop and I pulled the video and I watched it. And that was him.'

Aware of the shockwaves of hindsight that headed his way in the wake of his lenient treatment of Castro, Simone added, 'Well, the reality of life is everybody can do my job better than me. They all watched *NCIS* and *Cops* on TV. They all know all about police work. But the reality is, we did all the things that we could physically do and we're controlled by the Constitution. We just can't go booting somebody's door down because we suspect there may be a crime taking place. I drove by this house probably a thousand times and had no idea what was going on inside. Because if I had any idea, I certainly would have rectified it.'

Some legal experts are not so sure that Castro's arrest

might not have led to a search of his home that same day. One lawyer said, 'Listen, you have only got to look at that tape to see Castro is as nervous as all hell on the forecourt of the gas station. He is terrified because he is confronted with the power that could destroy him. Once at a police station, he could have let it all go. He was a man on the edge then, but his plan still had five years to run. Just the slightest bit of poking, of the right questioning at the cop shop, could have led to him spilling everything. So I think, in that sense, Mr Simone is being a little defensive in saying that it wouldn't have led to a search of his house. In and of itself, no. But it might have done. And five years of misery could have been spared these girls.'

Mr Simone is aware of this, and aware of the hatred that the community has for Castro. He added, 'As a police officer I was obliged to uphold the law and to stand up against vigilante justice. As a father of three daughters, knowing what I do now, my instincts would be to chain the guy to a telegraph pole and give baseball bats to the three fathers of these girls.'

But the fathers of these girls had only praise for Ariel, the 'good guy', who pounded the streets with them, handing out fliers on Amanda and Gina, even performing at one fundraiser to keep the memory of Gina alive – a favour for a father who called Ariel a friend.

Who was seen with his chubby arm around Gina's mother, her head on his chest, softly weeping as he whispered words of comfort to her?

Ariel, of course. The ultimate enemy within.

Community leader Khalid Samad said, 'We would put together a command centre for the searches and advertise it on TV and social media, and he came along. Sometimes his brothers, Pedro and Onil, took part in the searches too. We would hand out fliers in the area, and make sure people knew we were still looking for these girls. Ariel acted his part very well. He had us all fooled. He acted like he was concerned and had empathy. Of course, we know now that he had absolutely zero sympathy for these girls. That's for sure.'

In a further twist of the knife for his victims, he would insist they watch TV footage of the searches that were being conducted for them. He would laugh and joke as he saw the agony cross their faces, revel in the pain they felt for loved ones they feared they would never hug again. It was pure sadism on his part.

His daughter Angie was one of the regular visitors to the house during the long imprisonment years. She remembers how her father would 'take for ever' to answer the front door. 'Then he would give a hand signal and tell me to come around back instead,' she said. 'Once inside, me and my husband often had dinner with him. He played his music too loud but he was a musician, and I figured that's what he likes. But sometimes during dinner he would disappear upstairs and give no explanation about what he was doing. Once, I asked him if I could go upstairs and look at my old room, you know, the one I had growing up. "Oh, honey, there's so much junk up there. You don't want to go up there," he said. I didn't think any more about it. Certainly didn't think that there were women locked up in my room. I just thought he was messy, a pack rat, and let it go.

'Now? He is dead to me. He is the most evil, vile, demonic criminal in the world. I always saw Daddy as a friendly, caring, doting man, but now I'll never speak to him again. It is only with hindsight that I can look back and see the things that I thought were normal in his house all that time were not normal at all. He always wanted to stay close to home. Sometimes my husband and me would make plans that meant him going some ways from the house, and we would have to cancel them because he said he couldn't go far. Now we know why.

'And to think that he would go to the vigils for these girls, would hand out fliers on the street. Now I am sick to my stomach about my father's actions. For him to go to the vigils, to show these girls the footage of their parents' pleas for their return, to rape, starve and beat innocent human beings . . . I am disgusted.'

Ariel Castro proved himself a master of deception time after time. But when it unravelled, it happened at high velocity, a decade into his kidnap scheme, when his illicit baby daughter was heading for her sixth birthday. Again, it was outside forces – the things over which he had no control – which undermined the ultimate control freak. In his case, the turning point in his plan came when he was dismissed on 6 November 2012 for leaving his bus parked outside a school and walking home.

Down the years he had picked up numerous points for traffic violations. According to city records:

- On 13 July 1995: Parking near a kerb/handi-capped parking area. Castro pleaded guilty and was slapped with a $55 fine and court costs.
- On 13 September 2000: He ran a stop sign while displaying the wrong licence plate. He pleaded no contest in the case. He was fined, including court costs, $245 and found not guilty on the licence-plate allegation. He was assessed two points on his driving record for the stop sign.
- On 29 January 2001: He was hit with a charge of failure to obey a traffic device. He was found guilty, paid $95 and accrued two more points on his record.
- On 23 February 2004: Suspension action taken by the state because of the points mounting up on his licence. Castro immediately appealed and in March was granted temporary privileges for three months, from 11 March to 21 June. He paid a fine of $66.
- On 11 July 2005: He was cited for excess noise and emissions from his car and operating a vehicle with improper windshield glass. He was found not guilty on the emissions charge and guilty on the glass. He paid $285.
- On 20 June 2008: He was cited for lack of proper licence and improper glass. Both charges were dismissed.

Critics are still demanding to know why so few back-ground checks were carried out on Castro when he was first hired as a school bus driver. As detailed previously, he was suspended a total of three times: once for making an illegal U-turn with a bus full of children, once for using a vehicle to go shopping, and once when he left a male student on a bus and verbally abused him as he went off to grab a fast-food lunch at a Wendy's restaurant. 'Lay down, bitch,' he told the frightened boy.

Even that didn't get him sacked.

But the tipping point came eight years later, when he abandoned his vehicle.

Told he was facing being fired, he wrote to the school district, saying: 'I went home to rest. I've been helping depot with many routes that needed coverage. I felt tired all day.'

It cut no ice. He was gone.

And losing the structure of his day job, along with the money he so desperately needed, trapped him in a vortex of despair. He didn't know it, but he had become like Josef Fritzl in his longing for a way out of the prison he had built for himself.

As Fritzl aged and his daughter remained trapped beneath his feet, with two sons and a daughter growing up in the Austrian dungeon, he sought ways to bring his secret life to an end. Some of his thoughts were dark indeed – they even included murdering all those he had made suffer. He was bad, not mad, and knew that no one in society would ever understand the forces which had compelled him to create a parallel family in the rock and earth beneath his house. He began to fret and worry about how to bring it all to a conclusion that would keep him, and his petty reputation in Austrian society, intact. These were also the concerns which gnawed at Ariel Castro as the dynamic in the house began to change with the loss of his job.

Suddenly, Castro – who was never far from home but was certainly never in it all the time – found himself cooped up with his 'family' 24/7. He was in a flimsy house, where floorboards creaked and a young girl cried, where the smell of human waste was often overpowering and demands were made on him like never before. When driving the bus he was able to detach himself from his cooped-up sex-and-violence objects, fantasize about them during the hours when he was at work and come home to prey upon them at his leisure. But now, in his macho image of himself, he was nothing better than an *ama de casa* – a housewife.

An investigator close to the case told the author of this book, 'The period between November 2012 and May 2013 saw a rapid disintegration in his self-belief and his self-worth. He still made a little money while gigging for local bands, but his pay cheque had gone. He had nothing to get up in the morning for, and he hated it. He hated feeling like this impotent head of a family that he had convinced himself loved and needed him. The psychological bludgeoning the girls took during their incarceration certainly bound them to him, but if he had opened the door and invited them all to take a walk, they would have done so. Of course he couldn't do that, but he needed a solution because money was running out and he was falling behind with bill payments – property taxes, insurance for his bikes and his vehicles. By the time of his arrest he owed a little over $2,500 in mortgage arrears. He was

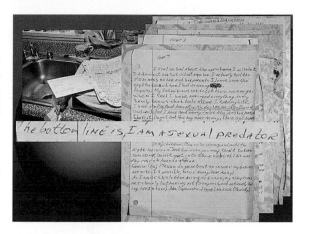

18. The scrawled letter written by Castro – two days after he had abducted Gina DeJesus on 2 April 2004 – in which he confessed: 'I am a sexual predator.'

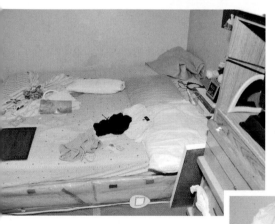

19. The bedroom of Michelle Knight, and later Gina DeJesus. The room measured a claustrophobic 6 feet by 6 feet and there was no bed, just a mattress on the floor.

20. One of the boarded-up bedroom windows. With no fresh air and little natural light, the women developed terrible vitamin deficiencies.

21. More than 92 pounds (42 kilos) of chains were found by officers in the house, which Castro used to restrain the three women.

22. A home-made alarm rigged to the back of an inside door in the house.

23. The single bathroom, which the women were given access to only a few times a week.

24. The picture wall in Jocelyn's room, with Disney film posters and schoolwork hung up.

25. The little girl kept stuffed animals lined up on the bed she shared with her mother.

26. Aurora Marti, pictured with her son Javier, who lived opposite Ariel Castro and was the first person on the porch when Amanda Berry cried for help.

27. Charles Ramsey, who claimed he found Gina DeJesus and Amanda Berry, speaking to the press on 6 May 2013 on Seymour Avenue.

28. Cleveland police officer Anthony Espada was one of the first officers at the scene when the three long-missing women were discovered.

29. The telegraph pole at West 105th Street and Lorain where Gina DeJesus went missing, with messages of thanks after she was found alive.

30. FBI agent Vicki Anderson, who ran the Castro case
in Cleveland.

31. Cuyahoga County
Prosecutor Timothy
J. McGinty, speaking during
a press conference on 9 May
2013 in Cleveland, Ohio.
Bail was set at $8 million
for Ariel Castro.

32. The courthouse and prison where Ariel Castro was held in downtown Cleveland, Ohio, while awaiting his trial.

33. Ariel Castro appeared with his attorneys for a pre-trial hearing in Cuyahoga County Common Pleas Court on 19 June 2013.

Dear Commander Sulzer, Officers
and Staff,
You don't know how much I
appreciate all your time & work
collecting cards and gifts from people
for me and the other girls. I am
overwhelmed by the amount of
thoughts, love & prayers expressed by
complete strangers. It is comforting.
Life is tough, but, I'm tougher.
"Just when the caterpiller thought the
world was over, she became a butterfly."
Thanks! God Bless You,
Michelle Knight M-K-

34. Handwritten note by Michelle Knight
expressing her gratitude to the Cleveland
Police Department.

tapping people up all the time for loans because he had to bring in the food for four people – lousy food, past-sell-by-date food, cheap and un-nourishing fast food, but food all the same. The job was a symbol of respect to Castro, as well as giving order to his life.'

When it went, it was the beginning of the end for him.

During this period Castro admitted becoming unfocused, more erratic, unable to concentrate, whereas in the past he had micro-managed everything because it was vital for him to do so. As the money dwindled, he contemplated letting the women go. But he soon ruled that out because it would have meant life imprisonment for him. He never admitted it, but he also contemplated killing them all – at least, the shrinks think he did. Self-preservation was at the core of his actions.

An investigator said, 'He kinda knew that the game of hide and seek he was playing with society could not go on for ever. When the job went, these thoughts of what to do, how to handle the situation, became ever more pressing and closed in on him twenty-four hours a day. The women have spoken of an acceleration in his brutal treatment of them in the six months before they were freed. In an ideal world – that is to say, the ideal fantasy world of Ariel Castro – he would have liked to have kept just Jocelyn. He truly idolized her and there was never any mistreatment of her. But he knew he could only go on for so long, passing her off as a granddaughter, or the daughter of a friend. He was fast running out of options.'

Prosecutor Timothy McGinty would later acknowledge this, and would remark on how dangerous this time was becoming for the captives. He said, shortly before Castro was sentenced, 'In the end, he claims that he "gave them all a chance to escape" by leaving the door to Ms Berry and her child's room unlocked. The defendant admitted and realized this was a complicated double life that he was leading. He also admitted that he did not have an exit strategy, the consequences of which could have been even more horrific.'

Dr Nuccitelli has said that Castro's enforced time with his bizarre captive brood is a fascinating aspect to the case. 'Just think – after he gets canned, he now has to spend all his time in a house with three women and a child. It must have driven him crazy. He has constructed all sorts of fantasies about what sort of man he was, but at the pinnacle of it would have been his own ideal as breadwinner, carer, provider, father. In his twisted thinking, he would think that he was somehow "failing" his family and they would think less of him for it. Of course, they couldn't have cared less, but people like Castro always place themselves at the centre of the universe they inhabit. This was always about him, never about them. The school district that fired him may yet be the body that takes the ultimate credit for rescuing these three young women.'

While the suffering of the captives continues to be measured by the doctors treating them, the damage Castro inflicted on his community – poor, ragged at the edges, but a proud community nevertheless – is more difficult to gauge. Specialists say emotions of guilt will run through individuals and families for years, with many plagued by nightmares and self-recrimination. Why did we not do more to solve the case? Were we too complacent? Did we not care enough? What could we have done? How could we have called such a guy a friend? It will pit neighbour against neighbour, causing a lack of trust among many.

All because of the actions of one man, who hid among them wearing the face of a friend.

Some 2,300 people go missing in the USA every day, and most of these disappearances take place in heavily populated areas. But that is of little comfort to the people of the Cleveland barrio. To all, the abductees were the 'girls next door' and they hate the fact that Castro has made them hate themselves. Castro, with the chains and the restraints and the images of subterranean suffering, created his own Gothic nightmare of a suburbia in which his erstwhile friends and neighbours are still trapped.

There is no doubt that in the minds of locals he was a monster, the bogeyman, the stuff of evil incarnate. Yet this book has shown that he was a modest man who hated the fact, and so disguised his numerous inadequacies with the grandiose master plan to create a family on his own violent, warped terms. He had a modest house, modest job, modest prospects, modest clothes. Only in his psyche was he over-blown, supreme and, in his actions, cruel and demeaning.

The authorities have had to paint him as a formidable fiend in a bid not to seem too foolish in not having stopped him during more than a decade of depravity. That is why Cleveland's locals also regard him through a prism of dis-tilled evil because it helps them purge their collective guilt. He acted monstrously and the epithet 'monster' was applied to him instantly. But he was, at heart, an opportunist – one who chose women who were vulnerable and who might not be missed as much as, say, women kidnapped from the avenues lined by the multimillion-dollar homes edging on to the shores of Lake Erie. 'Monster' implies he was anti-human, a devil in human form. In reality, he was a five-and-dime sexual predator who took things to the next level because he could.

Fixated on his mother, corroded by a hatred of his father, his craving for a depraved domesticity with his captives mirrored that of Josef Fritzl and will resonate down the years as people struggle to find answers to the single question of why?

Binoy Kampmark, a lecturer at RMIT University in Melbourne, Australia, wrote:

> The paradox here is a simulation of total normality. No one questions because there is nothing to question. Violence is internalized and ritualized. The discovery of the deception is treated by way of an orgy of collective guilt and vengeful anger. Castro's behaviour was the mirror to a society that was simply deceiving itself. And it is precisely those which tend to be desperately in need of heroes.

Many people in America think the Castro case has stigmatized poor people – painting them as somehow indifferent, as if they could have done anything more to derail Castro years before he was stopped – putting back their cause by years.

New York writer Nancy McDermott expresses it thus:

There was shock of a different kind in America following the escape of Amanda Berry and the rescue of the other two women. Later that night, talk-show host Bill Maher pointed out that 'there are areas of Afghanistan or Pakistan called unincorporated regions' which are 'lawless' and 'out of control' he said. The Cleveland kidnapping scandal suggests there are also 'unincorporated areas of America where we don't go', he continued. Though Maher probably meant well, he inadvertently betrayed his own prejudices about the life of America's working poor. Referring to the man who helped rescue Amanda Berry and who became an internet sensation as a result, Maher said, 'You saw that Charles Ramsey guy saying, "I was eatin' my McDonald's," and you get the feeling that, "My McDonald's," he eats there every day.' Perhaps he does. So what?

Maher's idea of 'unincorporated areas' was echoed in much of the coverage of the kidnappings. Only in a blighted neighbourhood could a monster like Castro go undetected, commentators implied. Only in a place like West Cleveland would a 911 dispatcher fob off a frantic Amanda Berry with the words, 'We're going to send them [the police] as soon as we get a car open.' The undertone of some of the coverage seems to be: if only the abductions of Knight, Berry and DeJesus had happened in an affluent suburb, maybe more people would have been suspicious of a house with boarded-up windows. If only the families of the women had had the wherewithal to mobilize the media more efficiently, the women might have been found sooner. In short, almost every aspect of this story could, it seemed, be put down to the fact that it took place in a poor neighbourhood.

This focus on inequality is reminiscent of the writings of Victorian reformers, who believed that the squalor of slums reflected the character of the slums' inhabitants. But unlike their nineteenth-century predecessors, today's media do not see moral corruption in West Cleveland so much as incompetence, ineptitude and gullibility; media outlets make sweeping assumptions about Cleveland, portraying the people in Castro's neighbourhood as passive and powerless.

The worst thing about this rather elitist approach is that it has blinded commentators and others to the positive aspects of this story. For instance, according to Rachel Dissell, a reporter who covered the disappearances for the Cleveland newspaper *The Plain Dealer*, in the case of the younger girls who were kidnapped there was actually 'a lot of attention from the local media', and 'people followed the case for years'. There was also attention from the police and FBI, she says. Moreover, the families organized searches and worked tirelessly to find their missing loved ones. They held vigils every year and continued to put up flyers around the neighbourhood.

The West Cleveland neighbourhood, which the *Huffington Post* describes as the sort of place where 'furniture is rentable, tattoos adorn everyone from teens to grandmas, and you might encounter a pig in a backyard or two', is certainly shabby and run-down. But its residents, if not exactly trusting, still maintain a sense of connection with their neighbours and extended family. Many came out to help look for Gina DeJesus. And yes, many of them knew Ariel Castro, in the sense of saying 'hello' to him in that casual way neighbours do. That is because, by most accounts, Castro seemed just like everyone else.

It is understandable that the residents of Seymour lament that they did not recognize the signs that something was amiss with Castro. Some take the view that the residents were too trusting. Others believe it shows that they should be more involved in one another's lives. But there is no reason to believe that a man who hid a terrible secret from his family and closest friends for years would be unable to do the same in a different neighbourhood. The truth may be far simpler: no one recognized the signs that Castro was a monster because there were no signs to see.

6. Endgame

Monsters make mistakes.

Admittedly, they are programmed not to – primed, as they are, to exist on a level of tension, fear and alertness most mortals outside of bomb disposal teams or special forces battalions never experience – but mistakes are inevitable. Minor mistakes brought down the two most notorious kidnappers of recent years: Wolfgang Priklopil and Josef Fritzl.

Priklopil, the kidnapper of Natascha Kampusch, groomed the schoolgirl to love him. She was with him in the garden outside his home, with its specially constructed cellar-dungeon, on the afternoon of 23 August 2006. He was allowing her to assist him in the vacuuming of his precious BMW car. Suddenly, at 12.53 p.m. his mobile phone rang. Removing it from his pocket, he turned his back for a split second. It was enough. Natascha Kampusch, then eighteen and determined not to spend her adult life as the cat's paw of this deviant who stole her childhood and much else besides, ran from 60 Heinestrasse in Strasshof-an-der-Nordbahn outside the Austrian capital, and never looked back. By the evening of that day her captor would be dead – decapitated beneath the wheels of a local train – and her ordeal of 3,096 days would be over. All thanks to a telephone call.

Josef Fritzl's mistake was in thinking that he would be believed above all others, that his word was law. After twenty-four years of keeping his daughter locked in a rat-infested secret cellar carved beneath his home in Amstetten, Austria, and protected by multiple sealed doors, a chink of humanity broke through the carapace of cruelty with which he had surrounded himself. Three of the six incest children borne by Elisabeth during her rape ordeal lived in the cellar all their lives, including the eldest, Kerstin. In April 2008 she fell desperately ill and the old jailer, believing she would die if he did not act – which would have been the case – removed her and took her to a local hospital. He lied to staff that she was the daughter of his own daughter, who had run away to join a secret sect and had dumped the child back on his door-step because she could no longer cope with her.

Doctors used to the most fearful conditions of the human body were astonished at the sight of a nineteen-year-old woman with few teeth, hair that came away in chunks and a chronic vitamin D deficiency. It was as though she had never seen sunlight. Which, of course, she hadn't.

Fritzl gambled that he could still control Elisabeth, that she would lie about her troglodyte life, and so he allowed her to visit Kerstin as she lay gravely ill. And that was the blunder which ended his reign of terror and rape. Police were waiting for Elisabeth, determined to charge her with the most atrocious neglect of another person they had ever seen. Both she and her father were taken to the local police station where detectives waited to quiz her. 'I can tell you another story,' she said, and did so, reducing hardened lawmen to tears as they filled up notebook after notebook with details of the depravities she had endured at the hands of her own father.

He rose to greet them as they came out of the room, expecting to be told he could go back to his comfortable life and ordered existence, as if nothing had happened. When the handcuffs went on instead, he was dumbfounded. If only he hadn't allowed Elisabeth to visit Kerstin, everything would have been different. He can ponder his error for the rest of his life as he sits in the Stein Prison for psychiatric criminals in Austria, assured that he will never walk away from its confines.

So it was with Ariel Castro. His world, too, ended not with a bang but a whimper which turned into a scream and, finally, morphed into a frantic emergency call for help that brought the whole of his rotten scheme crashing down. And all because he forgot to secure one little door.

It was to become the portal to freedom for his victims, and the gateway through which a stunned and horrified world would gaze in disbelief.

For the inmates at 2207 Seymour Avenue the day of 6 May 2013 had begun in the same depressing manner as all the other days of their imprisonment. They had coffee delivered to their cells. They averted their eyes when Castro came in to check on them. But on this day, the doors to the bedrooms were not locked. If the birth of Jocelyn saved the women on so many levels – spiritually, emotionally, psychologically – it was her interaction with their jailer that was to rescue them all on a day that started like every other one they had endured. For days, weeks – he couldn't exactly remember – the little girl, the one person in that house he treated with the dignity she deserved, had begged him to 'stop locking all the doors in the house'. One newspaper summed it up in a report after it was all over: 'He treated the girls like animals but he idolized his daughter.' This simple human emotion of love was to be his downfall. He did what his precious little princess wanted. He also kept the chains off their legs on this, the day of days. And in pleasing her, he condemned himself to discovery and, ultimately, death. 'I know I let my guard down,' he would later tell police in an interrogation room, in what was something of an understatement.

And so they heard his fourteen footfalls on the stairs on the way up and on the way down. They heard the sounds of him shuffling about in the living room and kitchen, the Spanish-language radio station playing, a few vague noises of cars passing and children shouting in the street outside. Their collective hearing had become acute during the years of captivity – honed, as it was, to detect when their tormentor might be approaching or leaving. It came around to lunchtime, the time when he departed. They heard the locks shift and then the silence fell. Later, he returned and, in the early evening, readied himself to depart once more for their junk-food dinners.

But there was a change. It was the absence of a single sound that alerted the women to the fact that something different, potentially life changing, had occurred. They heard the shutting of the inside door leading to the porch . . . but not its locking. They did not hear the mechanism which slid the mortise levers into place.

The house was silent. But they remained frozen, too petrified to move. Even though they knew they had only a few seconds to make a decision, they were too scared to do anything. Too often they had ventured out of their cells when Castro left the house to see if there was a way out. Sometimes he lay in wait for them and would beat them mercilessly, tie them up and starve them for days afterwards in retribution. Other times he told them the doors were booby-trapped and they would die if they attempted to escape. Yet this was the time, and this was the place, for action.

And it came through the bravery of Jocelyn.

While Castro doted on her, took her out and swore her to secrecy about her life in the house, the little girl had matured beyond her years and the vain, self-obsessed and self-aggrandizing bully that was her father failed to notice it. She instinctively knew that the life she led with Amanda and the 'other ladies' was not on the level – and neither was the man who kept them there. She ate his ice cream, she kept his secrets about the others in the house. But she knew right from wrong because her mother had taught it to her when she wasn't being raped or starved or beaten by the man who held their fate in his calloused hands.

It was Jocelyn, according to investigators, who had descended the stairs shortly before Castro left the house, who had chatted to him and noticed that the front door leading to the porch screen door had not been locked. It was she who returned to the frightened sisterhood upstairs to say, 'The front door's open and he's gone away. He's gone to Grandma's,' which was where he went to collect his brother.

This lost female group, a sorority forged in adversity whose shared suffering had kept them alive and given them hope, nourishing them in their darkest moments, screamed out for salvation. It fell on Amanda Berry to make the dramatic bid for freedom because the others were simply too cowed to move. This was the ultimate roll of the dice, the last chance to get away from the filth, degradation, pain and humiliation that their captor had heaped upon them. Amanda made the journey down the stairs with Jocelyn and, with the hopes and prayers of her fellow inmates of 2207 Seymour Avenue, she hesitantly crept towards the unlocked door.

As a police officer close to the case remarked, 'Castro probably wishes he had never fathered that child in some ways. It gave Amanda a reason to live and a reason to hope. She would have been as zombified as the others, were it not for her daughter. Castro thought he was master of everything but not even his cunning could factor in simple human bonds like that between a mother and a daughter. He was a monster – and a fool.'

Amanda slowly crooked her head round and saw the chink of light from where the door had sprung open. Their tormentor had indeed failed to secure it. She shouted up the stairs, 'It's open! It's open! I'm going for it!' She raced for the open door, pushed on the locked iron door outside that prevented her from stepping out on to the deck and yelled for all she was worth.

Above everything, above her concern for the other women and for herself, she did it for Jocelyn. She had seen the marked increase in the volatile behaviour of Castro in the months since he had lost his job. She sensed a seismic shift in the master's moods. She feared for her daughter, for the mind games he played with her. The fear she had for Jocelyn's future in this toxic house suddenly overcame the fear that Castro had inculcated in them all.

'This was a moment of enormous courage,' said former FBI hostage negotiator Clint Van Zandt. 'What she and the others suffered, it was like being prisoners of war. You have to make up your mind to survive, and you draw strength from the people around you – you draw strength from their ability to survive. If she can survive, I can survive. They probably drew some strength from each other. Berry beat the odds. On that day when Castro left to go to McDonald's, she realized that her captor had forgotten to lock the front door and seized the moment. I think that Amanda's maternal instinct may have made the difference. I think part of it was something concerning her child. She had more than herself to think of. It's difficult to comprehend the paralysing fear Berry had to overcome in order to escape – a fear all three of Castro's victims likely endured. It was an act of amazing fortitude after so many years of being beaten down.

'When police arrived the other two didn't run, and there is a reason for that. They were likely conditioned not to escape. There are psychological chains and restraints that are so much stronger than any steel chain or handcuff. I think they gave up the idea of escape because they had to consider the price they would pay if they didn't succeed. You do the cost–benefit analysis in a situation like that.'

A man called Charles Ramsey, who is still enjoying his Warhol moment in the media spotlight, was a supremely ironic knight in shining armour, the man who claimed all the credit for what was in essence a community effort in freeing the women. He has told the world that he was the first on the scene, he alone was the man who kicked in the door, he was the one who helped Amanda and her daughter struggle to freedom. It was a good story, but untrue.

What was true about the McDonald's-munching man – a man who had a way with street talk that appealed to middle-class folks who had never heard it before outside of Hollywood movies – was that he was himself a serial female abuser. Charles Ramsey was convicted three times of domestic violence against his wife, Rochelle. Ramsey's first domestic violence charge came in February 1997. He entered a no contest plea a year later and was found guilty of the count by a Cleveland Municipal Court judge. While waiting to be sentenced he was again arrested for domestic violence. He was arrested a third time in July 1998 as the subject of an arrest warrant issued in connection with his failure to appear for a court hearing in the first domestic violence case. As a result, he was jailed for violating the terms of his release. Ramsey subsequently entered a no contest plea to the second case and was, again, found guilty by a Cleveland judge. The domestic violence cases were consolidated in August 1998, when Ramsey was ordered to serve six months in jail, placed on five years' probation, and directed to attend a domestic violence counselling programme. Ramsey was again arrested for domestic abuse in January 2003. He was subsequently indicted for felony 'domestic violence with prior conviction' – a reference to his previous abuse cases. The judge in the case issued a protective order covering his wife, the couple's daughter – then aged fifteen – and Rochelle's son from a previous relationship.

According to a Cleveland Heights Police Department report, Rochelle Ramsey twice dialled 911 to report that she was being attacked by her spouse.

'My husband is trying to kill me!' Rochelle yelled.

During one of the calls, a police operator noted, a male could be heard in the background saying exactly that: 'I'm going to kill you.'

When officers arrived at the Cleveland Heights home they shared, Rochelle was 'extremely shaken and crying and had a fresh cut on her face', police reported.

During questioning, Charles Ramsey blamed his wife's assault on a 'male in red sweatpants' who fled the home.

Rochelle, however, confirmed that she had been assaulted by her husband and that no other man had been in the apartment. Rochelle is now remarried after divorcing Ramsey in September 2003, while he was in the state prison. In her divorce complaint, Rochelle cited Ramsey – whom she married on Valentine's Day in 1995 – as guilty of 'gross neglect of duty and extreme cruelty'. Ramsey has also been convicted and served two separate one-year jail stretches for crimes associated with drug abuse, criminal trespassing and receiving stolen property, dating back to the early 1990s.

Ramsey, a 43-year-old dishwasher who weighs nearly seventeen stone, never claimed to be a hero or a saint living in the barrio. Flawed he most certainly is, and so was his story about his part in the downfall of Ariel Castro.

This is what actually unfolded.

It was a woman called Aurora Marti, who lived in the house opposite, who first saw Amanda and heard the screams of the young girl. Despite a lifetime in America, Aurora speaks virtually no English. Through her son Javier she told the author, 'I just saw this terrified young girl, holding a kid in her arms and babbling away. I couldn't understand hardly anything so I went and got my neighbour Angel Cordero. He don't speak much English either, but we knew enough to know that this girl needed help and Angel started to kick the door down. It was only after he had managed to boot half the door off that Ramsey sauntered over and helped kick the last bit away. But don't believe all the hype about him being the saviour. He's just a big mouth.'

His big mouth, in fact, was on the telephone to emergency services at the same time as Amanda, freed after she rolled under the broken door with Jocelyn in her arms, was on another phone to the 911 emergency dispatcher at a neighbour's house. Ramsey's call at 5.50 p.m. and his subsequent expletive-laden interviews with the media have made him an unlikely star, but his part was small. The hyperbole, however, was massive. America, briefly, revelled in the bad-guy-done-good imagery as his phone call to cops went ballistic on the internet:

RAMSEY: I'm at 2207 Seymour, West 25th. Hey, check this out. I just came from McDonald's, right? I'm on my porch, eating my li'l food, right? This broad is tryin' to break out the fuckin' house next door to me. So, it's a bunch of people on the street right now and shit, so we like well, what's wrong? What's the problem? She like, 'This motherfucker done kidnapped me and my daughter and we been in this bitch.' She said her name was Linda Berry or some shit, I don't know who the fuck that is. I just moved over here, bro.

DISPATCHER: Sir, sir, sir, sir. You have to calm down and slow down. Is she still in the street?

RAMSEY: Yeah, I'm lookin' at her. She callin' y'all. She on another phone.

DISPATCHER: Is she black, white, or Hispanic?

RAMSEY: Uh, she white. But the baby look Hispanic.

DISPATCHER: OK, what is she wearing?

RAMSEY: Uh, white tank top, light blue, uh, sweatpants. Like a wife beater.

DISPATCHER: Do you know the address next door? That she said she was in?

RAMSEY: Yeah, 2207. I'm lookin' at it!

DISPATCHER: Oh, I thought that was your address.

RAMSEY: Nah, I'm smarter than that, bro. I'm telling you where the crime was.

DISPATCHER: And the people she said that did this? Do you know if they still in the house?

RAMSEY: I don't have a fuckin' clue, bro. I'm just standing here with my McDonald's.

DISPATCHER: Can you ask her if she needs an ambulance?

RAMSEY: [*To Berry: Do you need an ambulance? Or what?*]
   She need everything. She in a panic, bro. I think she
   been kidnapped so, you know, put yourself in her shoes.
DISPATCHER: We'll send the police out.
RAMSEY: There you go!

Amanda Berry spoke with the operator at 5.51:59 from
a phone across the street. Below is the transcript of that
call – her first words to a person, other than her kidnapper
and fellow captives, for ten years.

DISPATCHER: Cleveland 9-1-1.
BERRY: Hello, police. Help me. I'm Amanda Berry.
DISPATCHER: You need police, fire or ambulance?
BERRY: I need police.
DISPATCHER: OK. And what's going on there?
BERRY: I've been kidnapped. And I've been missing for
   ten years. And I'm here. I'm free now.
DISPATCHER: OK, and what's your address?
BERRY: 2207 Seymour Avenue.
DISPATCHER: 2207 Seymour? It looks like you're calling
   me from 2210.
BERRY: Huh?
DISPATCHER: It looks like you're calling me from 2210.
BERRY: I can't hear you.
DISPATCHER: It looks like you're calling me from
   2210 Seymour.
BERRY: Yeah. I'm with somebody. I'm using their phone.
DISPATCHER: OK. Stay there with those people. Talk to
   the police when they get there.

BERRY: OK. Uh . . . Uh.

DISPATCHER: OK. Talk to the police when they get there.

BERRY: OK. [*Pause*] Hello.

DISPATCHER: Yeah. Talk to the police when they get there.

BERRY: OK. Are they on their way right now? I need them now.

DISPATCHER: We're going to send them as soon as we get a car open.

BERRY: No. I need them now, before he gets back.

DISPATCHER: All right. We're sending them, OK?

BERRY: OK. I mean like . . .

DISPATCHER: Who's the guy you're trying . . . Who's the guy who went out?

BERRY: Uh. His name is Ariel Castro.

DISPATCHER: How old is he?

BERRY: He's like fifty-two.

DISPATCHER: All right . . .

BERRY: I'm Amanda Berry. I've been on the news for the last ten years.

DISPATCHER: OK. OK. I got that, dear. I already . . .

BERRY: [*Inaudible*]

DISPATCHER: Yeah. I've got that. And what was his name again?

BERRY: Ariel Castro.

DISPATCHER: And is he white, black or Hispanic?

BERRY: Hispanic.

DISPATCHER: What's he wearing?

BERRY: I don't know, because he's not here right now. That's how I got away.

DISPATCHER: When he left, what was he wearing?

BERRY: [*Inaudible*]

DISPATCHER: OK. The police are on the way. Talk to them when they get there.

BERRY: OK. I need . . . OK.

DISPATCHER: OK. I told you they were on their way. Talk to them when they get there, OK?

BERRY. All right. OK.

DISPATCHER: Thank you.

BERRY: Bye.

Angel Cordero held Jocelyn in his arms. He scrutinized Amanda.

'She appeared kind of ragged,' he later said. 'Her clothes were dirty, her teeth yellow and her hair was real messy. The kid looked very nervous, as though she had never seen anything outside the house before.'

Although, of course, she was the *only* one during the long years of captivity who had actually been let out.

Ramsey and Cordero and Jocelyn waited with Amanda next to them. The other two women were still upstairs, too traumatized to stir. Other neighbours gathered around them, their antennae twitching at the possible development of a 'scene'.

It seemed like an eternity.

Halfway across the world, in Syria, President Assad was being accused by the United Nations of using chemical weapons against his people in the escalating civil war. A hearing was scheduled in Boston for one of the suspects in the city's marathon bombings. And in Europe a debate was under way in the European parliament about reforming the Union's biofuels policy. But in Seymour Avenue, Cleveland, time moved at a glacial pace and the world was distilled down to one simple equation: would the police arrive before Ariel Castro returned home?

It was, for Amanda, like being 'buried in wet sand' as the minutes ticked by and still no police were on the scene. Afterwards, as he basked in the spotlight of adulation, that most unlikely of heroes, Charles Ramsey, said he 'tried to keep her cool' as they waited for the rescuers to come.

'I was eating my McDonald's when I heard this girl screaming,' he would later recount in his own inimitable style to the army of TV reporters who descended on the scene. 'I see this girl going nuts, trying to get out of her house, so I go on the porch and she says, help me get out, I've been here a long time. So I figured, y'know, it's a domestic violence dispute. So I open the door and we can't get in that way cos it won't move, a body can't fit through it, only your hand. So we kick the bottom and she comes out with a little girl and she says, "Call 911, my name is Amanda Berry." When she told me, it didn't register. And then when I was making the call to 911, I thought, I'm making the call to 911 for Amanda Berry and I thought this girl was dead! You know what I mean? And she got on the phone and said, yeah, this is me. And later detective Gregory Cooke says to me, "Charles, do you know who you rescued?"

'When they arrived Amanda said, "I ain't just the only one. There's more girls up in that house." So they go on up there, thirty or forty deep, and when they came out I thought it was just astonishing cos I thought they would come up with nothing. And my neighbour, he said to me, he got some big testicles to pull this off, bro, because we see this dude every day, and I mean every day. I been here a year, I barbecued with this dude, eat ribs with him, listen to salsa music with him, you see where I'm coming from, and I didn't have a clue that her or anybody else was in that house against their will, because how he is . . . he comes out to his backyard, plays with his dogs, tinkers with his cars and motorcycles and goes back in the house. So he's somebody that you look, and then you look away cos he's no doing anything but the average stuff, you know what I'm saying?

'There's nothing exciting about him, well, until today. Bro, I knew something was wrong when a pretty little white girl runs into a black man's arms. Something is wrong here . . . dead giveaway, dead giveaway. Either she homeless or she got problems. That's the only reason she run to a black man!'

The cavalry arrived within fifteen minutes and police were as stunned as the neighbours at what they discovered. With guns drawn, they smashed down the rest of the porch door and poured into the house.

Two women driving around the neighbourhood became witnesses to the historic rescue when they shot a video of the police storming the house. Jasmina Baldrich and Ashley Colon thought they were about to be pulled over when they noticed a police cruiser behind them, and turned on to Seymour Avenue. There, they witnessed the heavy police operation with officers approaching Castro's home. The spectacle prompted Miss Baldrich to take out her iPhone and start filming what was going on.

Miss Baldrich said, 'We just seen cops and then, out of nowhere, we see Amanda walking by saying, "I'm Amanda Berry."'

Like others in the community, Miss Baldrich was familiar with the Amanda Berry case. She was shocked to find the missing woman, clutching her six-year-old daughter.

'We knew like that,' she said, snapping her fingers. 'We both got goose bumps at the same time. We were shocked, we could not believe it but it clicked.'

Miss Colon added, 'People would die just to see these girls get saved, and we just happened to be there.'

Just happened to be there.

As did the neighbours, the postman, the policemen (over a thousand times), the friends, the band members – everyone who had never had an inkling. The atomized, look-away society. But now it was over, and the rubber-necking could begin.

When officers arrived at the home a sizeable crowd had already formed on the porch. The people parted to allow Amanda, clutching her child, to step forward.

'Just the emotion at that point of my partner confirming that it was Amanda . . . It was overwhelming,' police officer Anthony Espada recalled later. In a voice breaking with emotion, he went on, 'We figured he [Castro] might still be inside the house. She's pointing to the house. My partner immediately asked her if there was anybody else inside and she said yes, Gina DeJesus and another girl. And it was like another bombshell, with overwhelming force, hitting me. I believe I broadcast it that Gina might possibly be in the house. We immediately started running towards the house.

'As we were going up the steps it was so quiet, like peaceful, almost as if, OK, all we are going to do is clear this top floor, nobody is going to be there, and then just leave. Then we hear this scuffling, you know, something going on in this room, and I am waiting to see what was happening and then it was Michelle, she kind of just popped out into the doorway and paused there for a second. Within moments she came charging at me. She jumped on to me, saying, "You saved us, you saved us!" And I am holding on to her so tight . . . and then within a few seconds I see another girl come out of the bedroom. I just look at her. You could immediately tell who it is. Thinner. Again, I just needed confirmation. I asked her, what's your name, and she said, "My name is Georgina DeJesus." It was a very overwhelming moment. It took everything to hold myself together. You know, I have Michelle in my arms and you got Gina coming out. It was like one bombshell after another. That's when I broadcast it. We found them. Everybody was in the right place, it couldn't have got any better than that on that day.

'I don't feel like a hero, I am just glad I was there. Just making sure they were safe. I feel so happy for them. It goes through my mind every day, it is just unbelievable, the past ten, twelve years, what they went through. It keeps on playing back in my mind. I just picture us pulling up, seeing Amanda, couldn't believe it. I am just glad to have been a part of it. All the officers there on scene that day, everything just went so awesomely.'

Officer Barbara Johnson was initially back in the police station working on a report when she heard the call come in that Amanda Berry and the others might be in the house. 'In my head I was hoping that it was true,' she said. 'And all I knew was, I have to get over there fast. I wanted to be there if that was the case and they were inside. So I drove pretty fast, lights and sirens all the way. When I pulled up, I didn't see Amanda. I saw officers running towards the house and I got out of my car and ran right over there too. It seemed like an eternity but also quick at the same time. We didn't hear anything and then there was this pitter-patter of feet running across the floor towards us. When officer Espada put Michelle down she jumped up into my arms and held on to me and screamed, "Please don't let me go, please don't let me go."'

Fighting back tears, Johnson continued, 'I told her, hon, don't worry, I am not going to let you go. At that point Anthony was already interacting with the person I later learned was Gina DeJesus. He looked at me and the look on his face was like . . . wow. We found 'em! I cannot begin to tell you about the emotions that we felt. They're just unbelievable. And everything else was just a blur. It was surreal, just a feeling of the heaviness in the heart just lifted. And then came the next array of emotions. You didn't want to think about what had happened to them so you just kept on thinking positive. I just wanted to encourage them that they were safe now, that everything was going to be OK. I was just so focused on them, I can't even tell you what was happening outside. The girls were the heroes of this story. They fought every single day. They are the true heroes.'

Michael Tracy was the third officer who rescued the two remaining captives. He recognized Amanda Berry from her missing poster. She was standing outside the house waving at him as he pulled up in his police cruiser with blue lights flashing. 'I got out the car and said to her, "Is that you?" She was frantic, just like on the tape, things were pretty chaotic. Her little child was screaming and crying, it was just crazy what was going on. She gave us information on Ariel Castro, description, the vehicle that he might be driving. This time all the other cars are starting to arrive on the scene. I asked her if there was anybody else in the house and she said Gina DeJesus and another girl and I am like . . . *what?!* Words can't explain what was going through my head.

'We then set about searching the house. After going through the first floor and basement we went upstairs to see what was going on. I see my partner being hugged and Officer Johnson being hugged and then I see Gina DeJesus walk out the bedroom. I couldn't believe what I was seeing. I stopped in awe at what I was witnessing. It was just amazing. It was great for me and my partner and every other officer that was there. I kept up hope during the years, you know, I have a positive mental attitude. Now I was just happy and relieved that they were safe.

'Words cannot explain what was going through all our minds on that day. It was an overload of information. But finding those three girls, and Amanda's little girl, well, it was all simply amazing. All the cars from the second district were converging on the area and with the description of the vehicle and the suspect they were able to apprehend him at McDonald's.'

Stephen Anthony, head of the FBI, summed it all up when he said, 'Prayers have finally been answered. The nightmare is over. These three young ladies have provided us with the ultimate definition of survival and perseverance. The healing can now begin. Words can't describe the emotions being felt by all. Yes, law enforcement professionals do cry.'

The news flashed across the world, knocking Syria and the EU from the headlines as Cleveland Police Department dispatched cars across the city. One of them went to the home of Pedro Castro, who was taken away in handcuffs, a suspected accomplice to the crimes which had taken place at Seymour Avenue because of his frequent visits along with Onil. Arrested and taken downtown, the bewildered man had no idea what had befallen him, but he did manage to provide enough clues for police to seize his brothers a short time later.

Onil had been with Ariel at their mother's and first suspected something was wrong when, riding home with Ariel in his car, a police cruiser pulled them over. Ariel turned into a McDonald's parking lot at 32nd Street and Clark Avenue.

Onil later recalled, 'I said, "What did you do? Run a stop sign or a red light or something?" He says, "No, no. I don't know."'

When Onil asked the police officer why they were being pulled over, he said, 'All I can tell you is that you're in for some serious allegations.'

Both brothers went into custody downtown, where they were reunited with Pedro. Although the world found it hard to believe that siblings who went in and out of that house time after time after time down the years could know nothing about the crimes committed there, that turned out to be the case. Ultimately, the hapless brothers of Ariel Castro were saved from charges by the testimony of the captive girls.

One investigator on the case told the author, 'All three girls gave initial statements the next day. All three were asked, separately, if they had seen others, been abused by others, during the entire time they were there. And all of these girls cleared these brothers. They had seen no one. It was apparent from the get-go that we were not dealing with a conspiracy here but the plan of a single predator.'

There was some hard questioning of the Castro brothers to follow, as well as a court arraignment which highlighted their bewilderment at the same time as it seemed to illuminate the shame of Ariel. But after twenty-four hours they were free to go. Many find it hard to fathom how siblings, when told by their controlling brother not to go through this door or that door, would not do the exact opposite. But it seems they did as they were told, at the expense of the hidden victims in the house. They swapped prison jumpsuits for shirts and ties for one brief interview with CNN before retreating into a safer place, with the death threats from locals, and people further afield, still ringing in their ears. (They are now in hiding, with other family relatives, back in Pennsylvania.)

'I had no idea why we were being arrested,' said Onil. He confirmed, along with Pedro, that they saw Jocelyn during her mother's captivity, and that on two different occasions they witnessed Ariel bring the young girl to fast-food restaurants – once to a McDonald's and another time to Burger King. 'Each time, he said that the girl was his girlfriend's daughter,' said Onil.

Pedro said that, having arrived at the police station, he asked what he was being charged with and a police officer wrote the word 'kidnapping' on a piece of paper and handed it to him.

'I didn't have my reading glasses, I looked and I said, "Oh, open containers,"' he told a television audience of millions. 'She said, "No, read it again." And I said, "Oh! Kidnapping! What's this? Kidnapping?" I'm thinking, kidnapping. Who did I kidnap?'

Onil said his brother was contrite on their way to the police station. 'He goes, "Onil, I'm sorry. You didn't know nothing about this, Onil. I'm sorry, Onil." And that was it. And then that's when I broke down on my way over there. I said, "What did my brother do? What did he do?" And at the police station, when he walked past me, he goes, "Onil, you're never going to see me again. I love you, bro." And that was it. And he put his fist up for a bump.'

Both said they now consider their brother to be a 'monster'. They also said that one of the worst moments for them came when they realized that Gina DeJesus was one of the kidnapping victims, since they are friends with her father, Felix.

Pedro explained, 'I knew him for a long time and when I found out that Ariel had Gina, I just broke down, it's just shocking. Ariel, we know this guy for a long time and you got his daughter and you go round like nothing, you even went to the vigils, you had posters, you give his mama a hug and you got his daughter captive? But he always kept us in the kitchen, or we sat outside on the porch. We never got to go in the other rooms in the house. Sometimes we slept over in the kitchen but couldn't see into other rooms because Ariel had curtains up which he said were there to "save energy". The reason why we would go in the kitchen, because he had alcohol. And he would take me in the kitchen, give me a shot.'

Both brothers testified to the constant background chatter of a TV and radio, almost always on, drowning out the background noise which threatened to come through the thin walls and even thinner plasterboard ceiling at any time. They also said that since being cleared of any involvement in his crimes they had become the targets of vile internet death threats, vandalism to their property and even a break-in at one of their homes.

When asked if the public would always suspect they had a role in the kidnappings, they answered, 'Yes,' in unison.

Onil went on, 'The people out there who know me, they know that Onil Castro is not that person, has nothing to do with that — would never even think of something like that. I was a very liked person [before the arrest], never had any enemies. There is no reason for anybody to think that I would ever do something like that. It was a shock to all my friends. They couldn't believe it.'

Pedro Castro added, 'I couldn't never think of doing anything like that. If I knew that my brother was doing this, in a minute I would have called the cops, cos that ain't right. But yeah, it's going to haunt me down. Cos people are going to think Pedro had something to do with this and Pedro don't have anything to do with this.'

The pair also said that even though Castro was their brother, they would have had no hesitation in turning him in, had they known. 'If I knew, I would have reported it, brother or no brother,' added Onil. 'This monster is a goner. I hope he rots in that jail. I don't even want them to take his life like that. I want him to suffer in that jail to the last extent. I don't care if they even feed him.'

On the day that the first charges were levelled at Ariel Castro, the world witnessed an outpouring of sheer human joy on a grand scale in the neighbourhoods where the women had once lived, returning to homes they thought they would never see again. Amanda and Gina went home first, after being released from hospital following detailed medical check-ups. In Amanda's case, a DNA test proved beyond doubt that the little girl she had given birth to in captivity was fathered by Ariel Castro. Michelle, the punch-bag, stayed on in hospital, her hearing impaired and the bone structure of her face seriously damaged. She may need surgery in the years to come, as well as complex care for the internal injuries she suffered during her internment.

All the women were reportedly overwhelmed by the

tsunami of love and affection that was washing over them, not just from their fellow Clevelanders and Americans, but from people as far away as France, Australia, Canada and the UK, who had been sending in cash donations and offers of holidays, spa treatments and even furniture for new homes not yet chosen by the women. By the time Amanda Berry pulled into the street where her family lived, there was over $100,000 in a special account to be divided between the three women to pay for future therapies, living costs and other expenses. The women, of course, knew instinctively that their personal stories, told in their own words, were – are – worth a great deal more. Offers in the millions from the major US TV networks were laid on the table within hours of their freedom. But police and prosecutors implored them to keep their silence until Ariel Castro had had his final appointment with justice.

One prosecution source said, 'Within hours of Castro being arrested and the details being broadcast of what he had put these women through, his lawyers were bleating that it would be impossible for him to get a fair trial. To ensure that proceedings are wrapped up against him as swiftly and as fairly as possible, we begged these women not to speak out until the law was through with him. We did not want them saying anything that might be seized upon as being prejudicial to his case. And we were glad when they all agreed. They said that seeing him dealt with and put in a place where he could do no more harm to them was more important than dollars.'

The grimy rooms, disgusting food, soiled clothing – the fear, the humiliation and the terror – were forgotten for Amanda as an SUV driven by an FBI agent edged its way into the street she once called home. Hidden, crouching down, on the back seat was the little heroine Jocelyn, shielded from view by a relative. Yellow ribbons and blown-up photographs of Amanda – or 'Mandy', as her family call her – were all over the front porch. 'WELCOME HOME' said one giant banner above a forest of cuddly toys. Amanda and Jocelyn were shuffled into the house past a phalanx of well-wishers.

She left it to sister Beth Serrano to issue a brief statement on her behalf. 'I just want to say that we are so happy to have Amanda and her daughter home. I want to thank the media and the public for their support, but our family would request privacy so my sister, niece and I can have time to recover.'

Community leader Samad, president and chief executive of the non-profit Peace in the Hood, has spent more than two decades trying to head off trouble on the barrio's mean streets and has extensive contacts with local politicians. He visited the three women at hospital on the first night after their release and spoke to the media as the cheers of the crowds roared through the Cleveland streets.

'They were kept in a dungeon with chains. It was a sexual torture chamber run by this guy acting out his sick fantasies. They are extremely traumatized and they are slowly talking to investigators about what they went through, but nobody is rushing them at this stage. They are trying to reconnect the dots in their lives.'

One of the first dots Amanda joined up was with her family members down south, in Tennessee. Once inside the house, she called them to let them know she was glad to be back.

Her grandmother, Fern Gentry, of Elizabethton, asked her, 'Is the little girl your baby?'

'Yeah, she's my daughter, she was born at Christmas,' Amanda replied.

Many of her relatives, including her grandparents and father, now live in Tennessee. Some of Berry's younger cousins only know her through pictures and stories told by other family members.

'I'm glad to have you back,' grandmother Gentry said.

And Amanda replied, 'I'm glad to be back.'

Her father, John, said he never lost hope through his darkest days, always knowing his daughter was alive somewhere and would be returned to him one day. 'I didn't think she was dead. No, never. Keep hope. Keep hope. Don't give up till you know, because I never gave up. I knew her rough attitude would keep her going.'

Shortly after the celebrations, FBI agent Vicki Anderson, who was with Amanda and her daughter when she returned home to live with her sister, told a local TV station that she and the other victims were now under the care of the bureau's victim witness specialist. 'She continues to be in communication and getting them hooked up with the right resources. I'm just glad people are starting to leave them alone. I am sure that book and movie offers have been submitted to the attorneys and I'm glad that they have that representation so that they're not bombarded with that.'

Of the moment when Amanda was once again reunited with her family, she said, 'It was unbelievable.

The emotions that everybody felt . . . I think there were tears of joy. I think everybody's eyes were misty . . . she was hugging everybody and she was a little quiet. She was just overwhelmed.'

The same scenes were enacted at the home of Gina DeJesus. Hundreds of people blocked the street outside her family house, chanting, 'Gina! Gina!' and remembering the hundreds, the thousands of times they had seen her face on missing persons posters pinned up on lamp posts and tele-graph poles down the years. But most were not to see her on this day: Gina hid herself in a yellow hooded sweatshirt, only raising her hand in a jaunty victory salute, her thumb raised, to show that her spirit was still intact after all the years of captivity. Those who did manage to catch a glimpse of her as she slipped into the house said she looked thin and pale with her hair cropped closely to her head. Enveloped in the hug of a relative as she slipped into the home she feared she would never see again, Gina did not speak.

But her aunt, Sandra Ruiz, said the family was joyful at the return while needing time alone together. 'There's not enough words to say or express the joy that we feel at the return of our family member Gina. Thank you. I am ask-ing for your support, to be patient. Give us time and privacy to heal.'

Gina's father, Felix DeJesus, hugged family and friends while pumping his fists, with a huge smile across his face. 'I have a high and mighty God to give me the strength to fight and see this day,' he said. 'Too many kids these days come up missing. We always ask the question, how come I didn't see it? Why? Because we chose not to. As a community, you have to come out and watch the kids, even though you aren't their parent. Now I will become an activist to help find the rest of the kids who are missing. I'm the man who will be beside you.'

He stood next to Sandra as she begged townspeople to eschew any kind of vigilante justice in the wake of the women's freedom. 'Do not go retaliate against the family and suspect of this crime, because we are all God's family, we forgive them. But we won't forget. They will have to respond to the high and mighty. When we're ready, we will talk to you . . . There are not enough words to say or express how we feel about the return of Gina and Amanda and Michelle.'

Felix never gave up searching for his daughter and never lost hope. He thanked everyone who stood beside him over the past decade, adding, 'I had heart and soul to fight to see this day because I knew my daughter was out there alive.'

Apparently, the first thing Gina did was to ask for a tour of the house. 'She's happy, ecstatic to be home,' said Sandra.

'I just grabbed Gina and hugged her. I didn't want to let go. I still feel as if it's a dream. I still pinch myself,' said her mother, Nancy. 'There's no word to describe the beauty of just seeing them.' The women's release on 8 May came just ahead of Mother's Day in the States, and Gina's mom added, 'This is the best Mother's Day I could ever have.'

She also had forgiveness in her heart for the man who caused her a world of pain for ten long years, saying she refused to be consumed by hatred. Of Ariel Castro she

said, 'I would hug him and I would say, "God bless you."
I did not hate him. I forgave him years ago. I said it: I forgive whoever done it, just let her go.'

In researching this book, it became apparent among
the Puerto Rican community that every person knows
everyone else – or, if not, knows someone who does.
Nancy actually knew Ariel 'very well' after growing up in
the same neighbourhood. Her sister lives less than three
blocks away from the house where Gina was trapped, and
Ariel and Nancy would often bump into each other on the
street while her daughter was his prisoner.

Wearing the mask of the concerned citizen, he would
routinely say to her, 'How are you holding up?'

The character of Nancy dwarfs that of her daughter's
kidnapper and rapist. Finding compassion for him is, she
said, what God wants. 'When you start to hate a person, that eats you up. I don't have time for that. I have to
be, you know, I want to be happy, like I am now.' And she
said that, in the few conversations she had had with her
daughter in the time since her release, her faith in God
never wavered in the hellish lair of Ariel Castro. 'She
prayed to God and spoke to Him, like I did. And He was
listening.'

Ashley Harris, a young woman aged twenty-seven, was
among the crowd and brought her three children to witness the homecoming. She had participated in vigils and
searches for Gina down the years and said the day of her
homecoming was one of 'the happiest and saddest' of her
life: 'Happy that they are home, sad at what they endured.
God is good.'

A day after the homecoming, Gina's mother, Nancy, appeared on a top American TV news show to reveal more details of the girls' ordeal and the state of their minds once they were freed.

'They didn't want to be separated,' she said, intimating that the shared pain of what they had been enduring was what kept them alive and sane while in Castro's grip. 'Now they are doing great, it's working out good,' she went on, saying she was herself surprised at her daughter's ability to pull through. 'I knew she was strong – I think she's stronger than I am, to tell the truth. She is,' added Nancy. 'I feel so blessed and thankful to have her.'

But there was not such a happy ending for Michelle Knight, a troubled soul who had a fractured relationship with her family before she fell victim to Castro. She is in total seclusion, refusing to see her mother and grandmother.

According to a friend of Gina DeJesus' parents, they have offered to adopt Michelle. Lupe Collins said, 'She feels she was Georgina's sister for ten years in that house and she's still her sister now. They're going to take her in as their own family member and help her. Michelle doesn't want to go back to her own family because they abused her before she was kidnapped and they only want the money now.'

Michelle left the MetroHealth Medical Center five days after being freed and is now in hiding. The hospital said in a brief statement:

Michelle Knight is in good spirits and would like the community to know that she is extremely grateful for the outpouring of flowers and gifts. She is especially thankful for the Cleveland Courage Fund. She asks that everyone please continue to respect her privacy at this time.

Michelle was the longest of the three victims and the person who suffered most at Castro's hands. There was a brief reunion with her mother, Barbara, two days before she left the hospital but, according to local media reports, it was highly tense. Eventually, Michelle asked her mother to leave.

Asked whether they had managed to speak to Michelle, her grandmother, Deborah Knight, said, 'No, we haven't – on her request. She does not want to be seen by family.'

Michelle is apparently angry that her family thought she had run away because her son had been removed from her by social services shortly before she vanished.

'She feels they wrote her off, didn't look for her or keep the faith with her like the families of the other girls did while she was in captivity,' a family friend told the author of this book. 'The only one she has any time for is her brother Freddie.'

He managed to visit her once in hospital and said, 'Her skin was white as a ghost. She told me she was excited to start a new life.'

But it is apparent that, for Michelle, the ordeal is far from over.

Of all the messages of goodwill that touched the hearts of the women, one was from a fellow victim – kidnap ordeal survivor Jaycee Dugard. She said in a statement, after learning of the plight of the Ohio girls:

The human spirit is incredibly resilient. More than ever this reaffirms we should never give up hope. These individuals need the opportunity to heal and connect back into the world. This isn't who they are. It is only what happened to them.

Just a few short miles away from the wooden houses where reunions were being relived day after day, Ariel Castro found himself the new tenant of a cell in the County Jail, part of a massive courts-and-justice centre. In the same block prosecutors began preparing the case against him and indicated that they might well seek the death penalty for the miscarriages he inflicted upon Michelle Knight during the years she was his prisoner.

The arraignment of Castro was part of a set-piece legal strategy in which the state indicated its willingness to press for the maximum punishment – death – which allows for plea bargaining on the part of the defendant by confessing to most charges. Castro was told by his legal team from the outset that he should prepare himself for the death penalty if he was unprepared to admit to most of the charges against him. Cuyahoga County Prosecutor Timothy J. McGinty ratcheted up the stakes against Castro, threatening to pursue murder charges to their ultimate conclusion, all the while mindful of what legal experts were saying. They believed the lack of physical evidence – foetal material beaten from the body of Michelle – the likelihood of costly appeals and the fragility of the three women meant that a plea bargain was the way to go.

Terry Collins, the former director of the Ohio Department of Rehabilitation and Corrections, is a corrections veteran with thirty-two years' experience. He oversaw thirty-three executions during his career. He says his biggest concern in bringing the death penalty charges would have been the impact on the victims.

He explained, 'Death-penalty cases in Ohio usually drag on for twenty years or more before the execution is carried out, with appeals filed on top of appeals, all of which call for additional hearings, at which the victims are often called on to testify all over again, thus reliving their trauma year in and year out on the witness stand. And even when they are not needed to testify, the case will be screaming at them from newspaper headlines. For them, there really will be no end to it, no closure. They won't be able to escape it. And it isn't fair to repeatedly put them through all of this hell simply to satisfy our own blood lust. They deserve to be able to put this behind themselves as soon as possible, or they're going to be dying little by little right along with the monster the prosecutor is attempting to kill.'

Prosecutor McGinty was accused of grandstanding by some. One lawyer said, 'He knows that with no foetuses, and no exact time when they were aborted, the murder case will be very tough to prove. But he doesn't care. All he's concerned about is keeping the limelight on himself, for perhaps decades to come. This isn't about justice, and it's all very disgusting to watch.'

In Terry Collins' view, the prosecutor should have been happy in the knowledge that Castro would never be free again. 'Let's face it, if just one-tenth of the charges already filed against him prove true, there's simply no way he's ever getting out of prison. The judge will run the sentences consecutively. But the public just loves to get outraged and demand tougher and tougher sanctions, in addition to worse and worse treatment of the incarcerated, without any thought of consequences.'

Doug Berman, a law professor at Ohio State University, said the death penalty threat would ultimately turn the case into 'more of a spectacle than it already is'. He and others said the prosecution's biggest hurdle would be persuading a jury to return an aggravated murder conviction based on accusations that Castro caused one of the women to have a miscarriage. In order to secure such a conviction, McGinty would have to rely on a rarely used Ohio law from 1996 allowing for an aggravated murder charge in cases where a pregnancy is unlawfully terminated. Under Ohio law, the aggravated murder charges, coupled with kidnapping charges also brought against Castro, would allow McGinty to pursue the death penalty. But what if Michelle Knight wasn't pregnant and only thought she was? The FBI forensics teams that have swooped upon the house after the girls were freed, tearing up floorboards, plumbing pipes and much else besides in a bid to find the slightest trace of an aborted pregnancy, reportedly discovered nothing that would stand up under a legal spotlight.

'My assessment of it, absent any additional evidence, you're going to have reasonable doubt trying a case without a body and any physical evidence of how the crime occurred and the mechanism of death,' said Steve Dever, a former Assistant County Prosecutor in the office now occupied by McGinty.

'Jurors also might find it a leap to put someone to death for killing an unborn child,' said Richard Dieter, executive director of the Death Penalty Information Center in Washington, DC. 'While forcing a miscarriage is a serious crime, calling it murder jumps ahead and calls for a determination of when life begins.'

If the murder charges were allowed, it would not have been the first time in American legal history. In California, in 2002, Scott Peterson was sentenced to death after being convicted of first-degree murder for the death of his wife, Laci Peterson, and second-degree murder for the death of her eight-month-old foetus. Thirty-seven other states have similar 'foetal homicide' laws, mostly used to win convictions in car crashes in which pregnant women have died, or in cases involving attacks on mothers-to-be.

In 2011, a Franklin County man charged under Ohio's foetal homicide law was sentenced to thirteen years in jail for taking his pregnant girlfriend to an abortion clinic at gunpoint. In 2008, a Stark County jury convicted former police officer Bobby Cutts of killing his pregnant lover and their nearly full-term unborn daughter. But the court sentenced him to life in prison instead of a death sentence. Cutts unsuccessfully appealed the verdict on the grounds that a conviction of murder for the death of his lover was inconsistent with a conviction of aggravated murder for the death of the foetus. In June, barely a month after the Castro case became known, a Pennsylvanian abortion doctor convicted of killing babies born alive at his clinic avoided a possible death sentence by waiving his right to appeal in exchange for a sentence of life without parole.

Professor Berman said applying the death penalty to Castro would have pushed his case into 'uncharted territory socially and emotionally, not least because one of his victims was his daughter'. And he predicted that the appeals which would have been triggered by any capital case would run on for years and would continue 'to make headlines well into Amanda Berry's daughter's formative years. I mean, there are lawyers who are in kindergarten today who will be handling that case,' he predicted. He also said that the pursuit of a death-penalty trial would have presented enormous complications when it came to jury selection, asking whether the defence might seek to exclude any woman who has ever been pregnant, or whether the prosecutors would want only pro-life, anti-abortion jurors.

It is because of these crucial points, coupled with the need to keep the suffering of the victims to a minimum, that the case against Ariel Castro was finally decided in a back room, thrashed out among lawyers and then handed to a judge for a swift sentencing which saw the monster caged for the rest of his natural life.

On 19 June 2013 Castro appeared in Cuyahoga County Court at a pre-trial hearing just a week after he had been hit with 329 charges of rape, murder and kidnapping. Castro, who often chained his victims up in his house, was the one in chains in court, his wrists handcuffed and his ankles shackled. His head remained bowed for most of the proceedings, except when he answered a few 'yes' and 'no' questions for Judge Michael Russo.

His attorneys, Jaye Schlachet and Craig Weintraub, conceded in court that evidence for some of the 329 charges against their client was overwhelming. They said to reporters after the hearing that he was willing to plead guilty to some charges to spare the women from having to testify at the trial (leaving unsaid the fact that he would only do so, of course, in order to spare his own life too).

'It is not our intent to have the women do that,' said Mr Schlachet. 'There are definitely charges in this case we cannot dispute.' He said the door that had been left open by the prosecutor – regarding possible murder charges – was 'the most important aspect of the case for us, whether the death penalty is applicable'.

What is not in dispute is some of the more tangible physical evidence found at the Castro home and logged in the indictment. Case 574231-13-CR details on 142 pages the offences he committed and the 'criminal tools' he used to subjugate the women, while page after page chronicles the rapes they were forced to undergo. Incidentally, what is not contained in the indictment is Castro's curious 'suicide note' allegedly written in 2004 and found by FBI agents during their first search of his home as they scoured the place for forensic evidence of rapes and miscarriages.

While the complex legal tango went on, Castro paced the floor of his cell in a separate part of the complex from where the court is located. Sometimes he lay for hours upon his bed, drawing and writing. He showered regularly and brushed his teeth. While the house at Seymour Avenue was always filthy, he now seemingly developed an obsession for cleanliness – even asking for cleaning materials for his cell, which included a brush for his toilet. Described as polite, Castro initially had no TV and no magazines. The food was less than stellar: boiled eggs and grits (corn porridge) for breakfast; meat loaf for lunch; turkey roll for dinner.

Castro was allowed to talk with his two attorneys during daylight hours and made several phone calls to them. They said that he had found life in isolation 'extremely uncomfortable and unsettling'.

'It's not the Ritz-Carlton, and we wouldn't expect it to be the Ritz-Carlton. It's been difficult,' said Weintraub. He described Castro's cell as measuring 9 feet by 9 feet, containing a metal bed with a thin mattress covered in plastic, a metal sink, and some kind of mirror. When first incarcerated Castro walked around the cell naked, though he later covered up. He periodically asked guards for the time of day, looked out of the window and spent prolonged periods staring at the ceiling.

Castro's orange prison suit was composed of fibres that he could not tear, so he could not construct a noose to hang himself, while the buttons were made from a dissolvable chemical which prevented him swallowing them in a bid to choke himself. Although no longer on suicide watch after his first week in jail, the State of Ohio did not want to be cheated out of applying the full weight of the criminal law to Ariel Castro.

And so he waited.

7. The Reckoning and the Healing

The arrogance was barely tolerable to everyone who assembled in the courtroom. Shackled and bearded, it was Castro's third court appearance, on 3 July 2013, and the one at which he was pronounced sane enough to stand trial. He stunned lawyers, onlookers and the judge when he asked to see his daughter Jocelyn.

'I would like her to visit me, Your Honour,' he said.

Cuyahoga County Judge Michael Russo looked at him as if he had misheard the request, but then said firmly, 'I just think that would be inappropriate.'

Castro was subjected to an evaluation by specialists of the Court Psychiatric Clinic – inside the Justice Center, in downtown Cleveland, where he was being held – to gauge his fitness or otherwise to answer for his actions at 2207 Seymour Avenue. The tests were conducted before his court appearance on 3 July.

The judge ordered the tests because he wanted to make sure Castro fully comprehended the counts he faced, telling lawyers before he was arraigned, 'I want to make sure in this matter, as in many other matters, that the defendant understands the nature of the charges against him. I have to make sure that it will stand up in the future and also that he's afforded all his rights.'

Now that it had been decided that he could tell right from wrong, the legal battle centred on whether or not he would ultimately spend the rest of his life behind bars, or whether he might one day walk into the State of Ohio's death chamber.

The 'bad not mad' declaration was important both for the prosecutors seeking appropriate punishment for Castro, and also for an angry public which demands nothing less. Castro underwent a battery of tests to determine whether he was suffering any kind of mental illness that might have led him to commit the crimes he stood accused of. The determination of sanity started with a comprehensive psychiatric assessment where the presence of mental illness, substance abuse disorders, personality defects and intellectual dysfunctions were probed. During this process Castro's 'general assessment of functioning' (or GAF) score was determined. This is the score that is used as a general indicator of a person's ability to function in society and maintain self-efficacy.

Because of his ability to function for over a decade – to hold down a job while keeping the women captive, to show emotion and empathy for Jocelyn but not for Michelle, to be able to look after himself and the others – all this indicated he was a man in control of his faculties.

A source close to the investigation told the author, 'Almost always, the establishment of sanity focuses on this general question: Did the individual understand at the time he/she was committing a crime that what he/she was doing was wrong under the law? This may seem basic and obvious, but it's not. In Castro's case, what are known as the "4 Ds" – deviance, distress, dysfunction and danger – which define abnormality were found to be evident, but did not amount to a mental disorder. It might have been in his interests, for an easier ride in the system, to affect mental illness, learning disabilities or to appear intellectually challenged. But he neither affected it, nor would it have been in his interests. Inmates cannot continuously keep up the ruse, because they don't know what it really feels like to have any of those conditions, and eventually they make mistakes, as Castro would have done.

'Ultimately, it all boiled down to one thing: he recognized what he had done, recognized that within societal norms it was beyond the pale, and was not motivated by drugs, mental aberrations or impaired intellectual capacity in acting the way he did. He was sane, although he scored highly on the sadistic/aggressive scale in tests.

'The traits he displayed during interviews were depressive, antisocial, impulsive and passive-aggressive. He also said he had difficulties with anger and outbursts that stemmed from his childhood. And he also liked to present himself in a negative or pathological way and sought to intimidate and humiliate those he could, while wanting to fit in more broadly in society with those he could not control. The tests showed, above all else, a deep inability to feel empathy for others: life has always been about him, and still is. He has a grandiose opinion of himself, constructed over years as a defence against being made to feel worthless, stupid, unvalued by society. Taking the local children on bike rides, acting like the neighbourhood good guy was a way of him reinforcing these positive images of himself. Ultimately, he was diagnosed as being a weak man, unable to take people on equal terms, so he kidnapped vulnerable, weaker people.'

He even displayed remorse and repentance for his actions, but this is not uncommon. Repentance has been defined by Arizona State University professor Jeffrie Murphy as:

> ... the remorseful acceptance of responsibility for one's wrongful and harmful actions, the repudiation of the aspects of one's character that generated the actions, the resolve to do one's best to extirpate those aspects of one's character, and the resolve to atone or make amends for the harm that one has done.

Castro probably enhanced his opinion of himself as a 'good person' by the admission in interviews that he had 'done wrong'. He obviously felt remorse of a kind when the crimes were being committed – hence the half-baked suicide threat and the acknowledgement that he was a 'sexual predator'. None of this led to enduring changes in his thought processes or lasting reform in his conduct.

The psychological tests also had to determine whether the remorse was genuine. Deception is a major part of any skilled criminal's behavioural tool kit, and Castro honed his skills in this department over a decade. The experts looked for key 'tells' in Castro. Signs of fake remorse include swinging from one emotion to another very quickly – what is termed 'emotional turbulence' – and speaking with greater hesitation. He was scrutinized, studied and quizzed for over twelve hours in two-hour sessions lasting five days. It was decided he did feel remorse, genuine remorse, but that his feelings of power and self-aggrandizement were never far away.

In all important regards, he was found competent to stand trial. He knew what he did was wrong, but he still did it.

During his more formal police interrogation sessions, Castro denied having any more victims in his grip, or that women died in his basement and were disposed of. Michelle triggered a second search of the house, and of some derelict neighbouring properties, when she claimed there was another girl held there when she arrived but that this girl later 'disappeared'. Police thought this might have been another runaway, but Castro emphatically denied having abducted anyone else. He had achieved his magic number of three. He had no need of others.

He also discounted, as did police, the testimony of Elsie Cintron, who lives three houses away, who claimed her daughter saw a naked woman crawling in the backyard several years ago and called police. 'But they didn't take it seriously,' she said. Castro says he allowed the women out only on two or three occasions into his backyard, heavily disguised with wigs and make-up, just for some 'fresh air'.

Forensics are still combing a mountain of material taken from Castro's home, but they do not expect to find anything of value that will solve the cases of other girls who have gone missing in the Cleveland area.

And so, to sum up, Castro's acknowledgements during

his testing – his ability to recognize his own unlawful actions – pressured the prosecution into threatening to bring possible death-penalty charges against him. This only served to accelerate the pace at which his lawyers frantically worked to cut a deal to spare his life.

In jail, awaiting his appointment with justice, Castro was visited by 'family members'. These included his sister, Marisol, and his mother, Lillian, two women who continue to see only the good side of their sibling and son. A week before his competency hearing on 3 July, Judge Russo ordered restrictions to be placed on the calls and letters Castro was permitted while awaiting trial, declaring that he was only allowed to communicate with his mother and sister and that all telephone calls must be monitored by a jail official. He also said that three-way calls were prohibited and gave the authorities the right to terminate any telephone conversation in which someone other than his mother or sister could be heard on the line. In his jail-house talks with his mother he expressed 'profound sorrow', according to an official, 'for the shame I have brought you, Mama'. But it didn't take long for Castro to bring the sum of all his fears back on himself.

He was, apparently, terrified of what would happen if there was no death-penalty rap and he entered the general prison population. Rapists and child molesters – and Castro is both, given the age of Gina when he attacked her – are traditionally the scum of any penal institution, prey to ground glass in their food, boiling-hot water accidentally tipped over their heads, or a home-made blade sunk deep into their ribs. Castro knew, from the acres of newsprint and miles of TV film that his case had already generated, that his was a scalp any self-respecting con would want to claim, and he was terrified at the prospect. The only alternative would be a life spent – perpetually – in virtual solitary confinement. This has broken far stronger men than Ariel Castro. His torment was of concern to his mother, and one or two other family members, but most people were sickened by what he had done and did not lose sleep over it.

Things got a whole lot worse for Castro on 12 July when prosecutors, as they said they would, increased the charges against him from 329 counts to 977, including multiple rape, kidnapping and two counts of aggravated murder, relating to the miscarriages Michelle said she had suffered when he beat her after she fell pregnant. The indictment did not include charges that could carry the death sentence, but prosecutor Tim McGinty continued to say he was still 'reserving that option'. The new indictment also charged him with 512 counts of kidnapping, 446 counts of rape, seven counts of gross sexual imposition, six counts of felonious assault, three counts of child endangerment and one count of possessing criminal tools.

The 576-page indictment covered the period from August 2002, when the first girl disappeared, to May 2013, when the women were rescued. The first indictment covered only the period from August 2002 to February 2007, because more charges were to be added right up until the day of his trial or the day the defendant got to plead. It was an arbitrary stopping point, a legal breather for the Grand Jury considering the case and the prosecutors guiding them behind closed doors.

'Today's indictment moves us closer to resolution of this gruesome case,' McGinty said in a statement. 'Our investigation continues, as does our preparation for trial.'

But there was no trial. And the denouement for Castro was as the legal experts had predicted.

On 24 July, wearing the County Jail's prison jumpsuit for almost the last time, Castro appeared to confess to most charges, just twelve days before a scheduled trial date. In Cuyahoga County Common Pleas Court he acknowledged that he was willing to be sentenced to life, with its overkill rider of a 'minimum' of 1,000 years on top. He waived away all rights to a future appeal.

Prosecutor McGinty – who, sources said, would still have liked to see Castro executed – commented, 'He's never coming out except nailed in a box or in an ash can.' Later, he added, 'The guy is a fraud and a coward. Do not be fooled by this head-down, woe-to-me demeanour he has displayed since his arrest. He's a manipulator. He has no remorse and we will elaborate on that at sentencing on August first.' McGinty said the prosecution's presentation at sentencing would include experts on the Stockholm Syndrome. He said that the prosecution would also oppose any attempts by Castro to have visitation rights with Jocelyn when he was locked away in Ohio's state jail for good.

During the hearing, which lasted more than two hours, Castro pleaded guilty to 937 counts of the 977-count indictment, including two charges of aggravated murder in connection with terminating a pregnancy of Michelle's. Castro told Judge Michael Russo he understood he was giving up his rights, but said there were some things he did not comprehend 'because of my sexual problems through the years'.

Later, Castro said, 'My addiction to pornography and my sexual problem has really taken a toll on my mind.'

Judge Russo asked him if he understood that he would never again be a free man.

He replied, 'I do understand that . . . I pretty much knew I was going to get the book thrown at me.'

During the hearing Castro said he disagreed with language in the plea agreement that referred to him as a 'sexually violent predator' and he indicated that he had been a victim of sexual abuse as a child.

His attorney Craig Weintraub said he took the plea deal 'because the last thing he wanted to do was re-victimize these women who he actually had some relationship with despite how it started and despite the prolonged psychological impact on the relationship'.

Throughout the hearing Castro appeared lucid and seemed to understand the questions he was being asked – unlike in previous hearings during which he had stared at the ground.

'We really worked hard on him to make a better impression,' Schlachet said.

In a statement released by a law firm, his victims said:

Amanda, Gina, and Michelle are relieved by today's plea. They are satisfied by this resolution to the case, and are

looking forward to having these legal proceedings draw
to a final close in the near future. They continue to desire
their privacy. They do not wish to speak to the media or
anyone else, and they thank people for continuing to
respect their privacy as they grow stronger. They are
immensely grateful for the support they have received
from family, friends, and the donations to the Cleveland
Courage Fund.

The Castro plea bargain was a relief for everyone,
including the police officers who helped free the three
girls.

'This was the best thing to happen in this community,'
Police Commander Keith Sulzer said after the court hearing. 'The girls can put this behind them and move on with
their lives, and so can my officers who have been living
this case every day.'

Anthony Castro, the monster's tortured son, hopes he
can move on too, but he knows it will be difficult. He
appeared on the top-rated American TV show *Today*,
shortly after his father's plea bargain, to denounce him.

'I cannot express how happy I am that my father will
never be able to hurt anyone again. Behind bars is where
he belongs for the rest of his life. I have absolutely nothing to say to him. What he did still haunts me. I have the
same name as him and when I look in the mirror I see the
resemblance and I think about what he did and how hor-
rible it is and I am overcome with that.

'Growing up with him . . . he was incredibly strict, he had
a temper. I mean, he wasn't a monster 24/7 but if you

crossed him there would be consequences. Now I see he's been lying to his family for the past ten, eleven years at every possible turn. I have no trust in him. I can't see myself going to visit him and giving him the opportunity to face me and lie to me again. As a child I would cry myself to sleep because my legs were covered in welts from his belt and I had to watch my mom get beat up. No one should ever have to see their mom crumpled in a heap on the floor beaten.'

Castro's last appearance before the public – before he, too, was to vanish into the maw of the Ohio state prison system – lasted four hours on 1 August 2013. It was the formal seal on his sentencing agreement, struck the week before, and became a piece of moving legal theatre.

Michelle Knight, the woman who came out of his clutches the weakest and most abused, summoned up extraordinary amounts of courage to confront Castro in court. Michelle, who later listened to Castro try to paint a picture of love and happiness in the hell-house where she spent over ten years, spoke for herself, the world and the human spirit itself when she faced him.

'I missed my son every day. I wondered if I was ever going to see him again. He was only two and a half when I was taken. I would look inside my heart and see my son. I cried every night. I felt so alone. I worried about what might happen to the girls and me every day. The years turned into eternity. I knew nobody cared about me . . . Christmas was a most traumatic day because I didn't get to spend it with my son.

'Gina and I were a team. I never let her fall and she

never let me fall. My friendship with Gina is the only good thing to come from this situation. We said we'll all get out alive some day, and we did.

'I remember all of the times you came home talking about everyone else that did someone wrong. You acted like you weren't doing anything wrong. You said, "At least I didn't kill you." You took eleven years from my life, but I've got my life back. I spent eleven years in hell. Now your hell is just beginning. I will overcome all that happened, but you're going to face hell for eternity. From this moment on, I am *not* going to let you define me or affect who I am. I will live on but you will die a little more inside each day as you think of those eleven years and the atrocities you inflicted on us.

'What does God think of you hypocritically going to church each Sunday and then coming home to torture us? The death penalty would be the easy way out; you don't deserve that. We want you to spend the rest of your life in prison. I can forgive you but I'll never forget. With God's guidance, I'll prevail and help other victims who may have suffered at the hands of another. I know there's a lot of people going through hard times but they need someone to reach out a hand for them to hold and let them know they are being heard. After a long eleven years, I am being heard and it feels liberating.'

The court was shown photographs of the chaotic state of the house, strewn with more than 92 pounds of chains measuring 99 feet in length. Also shown were photos of the wigs Castro made his captives wear on the rare occasions when he allowed them to leave the house.

FBI special agent Andrew Burke said Castro turned his house 'into a prison by installing alarms and locking them into bedrooms and removing the doorknobs and boarding up the windows'. Castro kept a stash of cash hidden in a washing machine and he would humiliate his victims by throwing money at them 'for sex after he raped them'. And he admitted the veracity of the letter in which Castro confessed to being a 'sexual predator'.

Judge Michael Russo heard how Castro would take a handgun – unloaded, allegedly, but his captives did not know that – and challenge them to play Russian roulette. He heard details of how Castro mostly fed them on just one meagre meal a day, to sap their strength and keep them compliant. How he bound their ankles with heavy chains 'like slaves'. How they sweltered in their cells, which had no air coming in through the boarded-up windows. And how he raped, raped and raped again to satisfy his primitive urges.

When it came to his justification, everyone heard it, but no one was listening. Castro could have used his time in the dock to speak healing words, words of sorrow or repentance. Instead he embarked on a rambling speech of self-justification in which he painted himself, not the women, as the victim, claiming that the sexual ordeals he subjected them to were, in fact, consensual acts and that there was 'harmony' in the house.

'First of all, I am a very emotional person so I am gonna try and get it out. I was a victim of sex acts as a child,' Castro declared. 'The imprisonment was consensual. I've been a musician for a long time. To be a musician and to be a monster, I don't think I can handle that. I'm a happy person inside. I drove a school bus for twenty-one years. I did a very good job. Towards the end I started slacking off, trying to get fired, because I knew it was just too much. The job was too stressful and coming home to my situation, I just couldn't juggle both of them.'

With regard to his ex-wife, Grimilda, he laid the blame squarely on her for the terrible beatings he dished out. 'I was never abusive until I met her . . . They're saying I'm a wife beater, that's wrong. This happened because I couldn't get her to quiet down . . . She put her hands on me, and that's how I reacted, by putting my hands on her. I'm not a violent person. I drove a school bus, I was a musician, I had a family. I do have value for human life because every time I came home, I would be so glad for the situation.

'My daughter, she just made every day for me after she was born. She never saw any violence going on in that house . . . She'd probably say, "My dad is the best dad in the world." I'm a normal person, I'm just sick. I have an addiction, just like an alcoholic has an addiction. Alcoholics cannot control their addiction.

'Most of the sex that went on in the house and probably all of it was consensual. These allegations about being forceful on them, it's totally wrong. There were times they would ask me for sex. I did not prey on these women, I just acted on my sexual instincts because of my addiction . . . God as my witness, I never beat these women. I never tortured them.'

At this point he took the video of Amanda, seen at a

rap concert the previous weekend climbing on to the stage, as evidence of how well she had been treated. 'We had a lot of harmony going on in that home and if you've seen the YouTube video of Amanda this weekend, that proves that girl did not go through no torture . . . If that was true, do you think she would be out partying already and having fun? . . . All the victims are happy.'

Then, 'I just hope that the victims find it in their hearts to forgive me and to maybe do some research for people who have addictions so they can see how that addiction takes over their lives.'

Judge Russo, along with the attorneys, the prosecutors, the onlookers, the marshals and the reporters crammed into the court, was unmoved by Castro's words. He matter-of-factly handed down a sentence of life plus 1,000 years, which would ensure Castro's death in prison.

'Excuses don't take away the harm that's involved,' Russo said. 'You have extreme narcissism and it seems rather pervasive. There is no place in this city, there is no place in this country, indeed there is no place in this world for those like you who enslave others, who sexually assault others, those who brutalize others. For ten years you have preyed upon three young women, you subjected them to harsh and violent conduct. You felt you were dominating them but you were incorrect. You could not take away their dignity. Although they suffered terribly, Miss Knight, Miss DeJesus and Miss Berry could not give up hope. They have persevered; in fact, they have prevailed. These remarkable women again have their freedom, the most precious aspect of being in America.

'Mr Castro, you have forfeited that right. You now become a number with the Department of Rehabilitation and Corrections. You will be confined for the rest of your days.'

The little big man, the monster in an orange jumpsuit, the man who beat five babies from the stomach of Michelle Knight, who raped her in the aftermath of the birth of his baby, Jocelyn, shuffled off in chains to a life of confinement and unceasing anxiety in a prison system where people of his sort rank somewhere below a cockroach.

Outside the court, in the bright sunshine, the yellow ribbons tied to the trees and telephone poles around the homes of Michelle Knight, Amanda Berry and Gina DeJesus are faded, the missing persons posters bearing their images tattered and torn. People will gradually forget the horrors that have plunged Cleveland into the spotlight, making it briefly the epicentre of world news.

Seymour Avenue morphed overnight into the safest block in the city, perhaps in America. As the media frenzy built after the breakout, the house became a must-see attraction for society's ghoulish or just plain curious. Afraid that curiosity might lead to trespass of a crime scene still sheltering potential secrets and evidence, the authorities sent in a work crew to construct a chain-metal fence all around it, as well as two abandoned neighbouring properties bordering it. For good measure, the windows once sealed with plastic and chicken wire were covered from the outside with chipboard, and two policemen in two separate cars were posted outside the front and rear to guard the house around the clock.

The residents of Seymour Avenue have never felt so cared about.

The women continue to spend time with families who had become strangers, playing catch-up with a world that has passed them by: digital phones, broadband, speed dating, online banking. Just as each woman suffered in her own way, each is healing in her own way.

Michelle remains the Cinderella of the family – as she was when she was taken, as she was when she was captive – the one who stayed in hospital the longest because of her injuries, and who had no wish to return to a family she believed had forgotten all about her when she was missing. 'The Forgotten Abductee' the newspapers called her. While the balloons were released and the crowds cheered outside the homes of Amanda and Gina, Michelle seemed to slip off the consciousness radar once more, refusing to meet with her mother or grandmother, granting one hospital audience to her twin brother, Freddie, before slipping away to who knows where.

'Mentally, she is having a tougher time dealing with this tragedy than the others,' said one of her aunts. 'She was held the longest and she was treated the worst. She feels police brushed her case off because she was an adult, and she feels bitter. She wants Joey back and she wants her life back but I don't know where all this will end up.'

Her mother, Barbara Knight, has tried to mount a PR counter-offensive, claiming she never gave up hope, that she was instrumental in searching for her daughter. 'I just wish that my daughter would reach out and let me know that she's there,' said Barbara, who now lives in Florida. 'I don't want her to think that I forgot about her . . . Hopefully whatever happened between us, if something did, I hope it heals because I really want to take her back to Florida with me.'

Barbara is reportedly working with a lawyer to fight for access to Michelle. 'The most important thing of all is that Michelle finds happiness and comfort after this,' she added.

Michelle remains unconvinced and feels unloved.

Gina's mother, Nancy Ruiz, said in a TV interview that it initially took some time before Amanda, Gina and Michelle were OK being separated. 'For nine years, these three girls were all one another had,' she said.

But theirs was a society born out of circumstance, not friendship. In fact, they were parted just hours after the first two left hospital and it is unclear whether they have reconnected at all since then. Some reports said the prosecutors had forbidden them to talk, in case attorneys for Castro claimed a conspiracy and their evidence was tainted as a result, but they wouldn't comment on this.

For Amanda it is little Jocelyn – the saviour of her mother and, later, of them all – who comes first. Back at a family home devoid of her beloved mother, she wept as she sat with her daughter and opened up the piles of Christmas and birthday presents her mom bought for her during the early years of her captivity, before her mother passed away. The presents were her only link to a woman who, like her, gave her all for her daughter.

Amanda barely remembered her father when she was

incarcerated but, shortly after her release, she travelled to Tennessee to be with him and to show off the daughter who is her pride and joy. They do not have much time: he is dying of a pulmonary disease and may not live for another year. Amanda was pictured for the first time since before her abduction in the American supermarket tabloid the *National Enquirer*, in its edition of 1 July. The exclusive photos that accompanied the exclusive interview from her father, Johnny Berry, were made to look as if they had been taken without her being aware of a camera nearby. She is seen carrying a plate of food and sitting in a car. But this is a standard technique in magazines of this sort. A source told the author of this book that money exchanged hands for both photos and interview, while Amanda kept her silence at the behest of prosecutors before Castro was dealt with. There are few who would begrudge her.

The *Enquirer* story told how Amanda had not seen her father since before she was kidnapped in 2003 by Castro. The 'tearful reunion' took place, appropriately, over Father's Day weekend. 'Spending time with my daughter Amanda and my granddaughter was the best Father's Day ever,' he told the magazine.

The painful childhood had, it seemed, been forgotten – perhaps because, with her mother gone, Amanda needs someone, anyone, to cling to after her ordeal. Amanda, her daughter, Jocelyn, and Amanda's sister Beth Serrano made the eight-hour drive from Cleveland to Elizabethton, in Tennessee, where father and daughter spent five days getting reacquainted.

According to the *Enquirer*, Johnny said:

When Amanda came through my front door it was like a miracle. She started crying and ran up to me and we hugged for the first time in ten years. I had tears in my eyes the size of raindrops.

Man, I couldn't believe it. I didn't want to let her go. I told her, 'Bout time you got here!' That made her laugh. Then, finally, Amanda said to me the words I haven't heard from her in ten years, 'Happy Father's Day, Daddy.' And before I realized it, she slipped a beautiful silver ring on my finger that says: 'DAD'. I'm never going to take that ring off.

I thought I would be a bit nervous meeting Jocelyn but she just fit right in immediately. She gave me a hug and I instantly knew deep in my heart that she's a Berry. She has her mom's beauty, strength and intelligence. I said to her: 'Hi, Jocelyn, I'm your grandpa Johnny, and I love you.'

Johnny Berry said that Amanda wasn't ready to talk about the painful years she had spent as Castro's prisoner, but he called her a 'real survivor':

She's real strong. Her nickname as a kid was 'Commando Amando'. I brought my kids up tough, and Amanda is proof of that. I'm going to let her talk about it when she's ready. I'm just happy she's back home. I'm here for her and ready to help in any way I can.

Johnny said he wanted to make Amanda's first trip to visit him as comfortable as possible, so he fixed up her old bedroom as soon as he found out she was coming. He put some family photos on the wall and got her some beautiful flowers. 'I wanted everything to be perfect,' he said, organizing visits to other relations in the area and a small reunion party at a local campsite where they feasted on hot dogs, cheeseburgers and potato salad. And they surprised her with her favourite dessert – banana pudding. Johnny noted:

> Amanda is slowly getting her life back on track. She's getting her and her daughter's medical checkups completed and thinking about putting Jocelyn into school next year. Amanda is going to finish up her high school education and wants to eventually go to junior college. She's even painted her nails and dyed her hair blonde. She really can't make any major plans until the trial is over. Once it is, I'm hoping that she'll move down here to Elizabethton where she has tons of family.

He also said that Amanda felt a little 'trapped' from time to time as, pending the trial, she had to tell the FBI whenever she went anywhere, and was forbidden from contacting her fellow captives until after the proceedings. 'Amanda told me she's coming back to see me next month,' he added. 'I'm already counting the days.'

For Gina, the youngest victim, her family have formed a protective shell around her and appointed an attorney to handle the media offers. She managed to persuade her parents to allow her to adopt her captor's dog, a terrier mongrel called Lola. Therapists agree that it is a good thing for a trauma victim like Gina to have a pet, and Lola allows her to show empathy with another living creature which survived, with her, through part of those years. Gina formed a special bond with Lola in captivity – although, just as the withdrawal of food and TV was a form of punishment Castro practised, sometimes Lola was kept away from Gina for long periods in the house. At the time of writing this book, his other dogs – a chihuahua named Dina and a three-year-old Shih Tzu mix named Drake – were up for adoption.

Gina has spent her first weeks and months of freedom catching up with friends she last saw as a fourteen-year-old. One of them was Jessica Aponce, who walked part of the way home with her on the day that Castro offered her a ride.

'She called her mom and told her mom she was on her way home, and that's the last time I seen her,' Aponce said. 'I just can't wait to see her. I'm just so happy she's alive. It's been so many years that everybody was thinking she was dead.'

Other than that, she has enjoyed shopping trips, meals out, getting her nails manicured and having a proper 'hairdo'. She has also been relearning her mother tongue. Castro spoke only in English to her – and Michelle, her companion, spoke no Spanish – so she literally forgot the language she was brought up with. In between everything else, she has promised her family to be conversing with them by Christmas.

These are the normal, everyday things that link the survivors to a world of wonder but also strangeness that exists against the backdrop of their own tortured psyches. The question for them, for their families, for the doctors assigned to treat them, remains unanswered. Just how badly damaged are they? Physically, Michelle aside, the problems are not insurmountable: mild malnutrition and vitamin deficiencies. It is what is not seen – what lies inside the mind – that poses the challenges.

The two classic abduction-rape cases referred to throughout this work, those of Natascha Kampusch and Elisabeth Fritzl (both of which I chronicled in previous books), provide a framework for the experts when it comes to the healing process for the Cleveland trio. When Natascha Kampusch ran away from her kidnapper she focused on money above everything else. It was as if she knew her intrinsic value as a media commodity in the first steps she took after running away, hiding her face with her jacket when police arrived in case cameras were lurking. No one pushed Natascha in this direction; she followed this path of her own accord and, say experts, did not allow herself time to work through the confused feelings she experienced for her abductor.

Doctors spoke of a 'puzzle personality' whereby she oscillated between being eloquent and strong, when the situation demanded it, and being ill-mannered and insult-ing (more so towards women than towards men). Her body rebelled against the high-tension world of inter-views and fame that she threw herself into, causing her to constantly fall ill with high fevers. Her doctors advised her against the 'atmosphere of voyeurism and blunt profit-making' with which she chose to surround herself.

It made it more difficult for them to help her exorcize the ghost of Priklopil, whom she mourned and, on a certain level, still mourns to this day. He was her only contact during the crucially important years of her life when she changed from a girl into a woman. He was the person who brought her up, the master of everything.

'One must always bear in mind how ambivalent her position is. At times she might look and sound like a mature adult woman, while at other times she appears to be a ten-year-old little girl,' one of her carers said at the time. 'And I have no doubt that in some aspects of her personality she is really a ten-year-old girl. She did not go through the normal development phases like everyone else. She had no puberty or adolescence and, more importantly, she had no chance of interaction with other people. Except for that monstrous man who kept her imprisoned. She will definitely need therapy for years to come.'

Elisabeth Fritzl was, mentally, stronger than Natascha. She was eighteen when she vanished, and later emerged with six children to nurture. Aside from panic attacks at midnight, a sometimes obsessive need to shower and an inability to sleep in a house with doors – the home given to her by the Austrian state has none – she has recovered well from the nightmare of her stolen life. She poured everything into keeping the children healthy in the cellar and succumbed to her deranged father's every demand in order to keep them safe. She taught them respect, love and decent human values in a place where there were none.

Cellar children Kerstin, Stefan and Felix – the three

who lived all their lives underground with her – now have new names. Felix, like Jocelyn, was only six when he emerged from his subterranean captivity. He reduced the policeman who carried him to safety to tears when he suddenly pointed at the stars and asked, 'Does God live there?' At that age, more was possible in terms of damage control. He has virtually forgotten his life underground since being freed in April 2008. He is now a healthy eleven-year-old boy for whom memories of the underworld have receded. The cellar is but some vague recollection, chased away by new experiences and by happier and more colourful recent memories.

For Kerstin and Stefan, things have been more problematic. They had confused, toxic feelings towards their grandfather, the man who kept them underground but who also brought them treats, Christmas presents and clothes. The man who took their mother away to rape her, but who was never anything but kind towards them. In classic 'Stockholming' behaviour, they experienced feelings of guilt, which they directed at themselves, rather than revulsion towards him. Stockholm Syndrome is also sometimes discussed in reference to other situations with similar tensions, such as wife beating, child abuse cases and bride kidnapping. It was named after the robbery of Kreditbanken at Norrmalmstorg, in central Stockholm, Sweden, in which the bank robbers held bank employees hostage for six days in August 1973. After the captives were released unharmed, the police remarked on a curious phenomenon. The victims became emotionally attached to their victimizers, defending their captors after they were freed. The term was coined by the criminologist and psychiatrist Nils Bejerot, who assisted the police during the robbery.

The Fritzl clan also exhibited the classic signs of post-traumatic stress disorder. Long after they gained their freedom they preferred solitude and shunned social situations, precisely because they had never interacted with a single soul but their mother. They had terrible flashbacks of being in the cellar again, which would cause them to hyperventilate and sometimes pass out. They experienced constant sweating, shivering, pounding heart or intensive breathing. They suffered loss of memory and lack of concentration, anger and panic attacks, abnormally high stress levels when in unstressful situations and, worst of all, a constant sense of guilt, betrayal and mistrust. As well as medications, the Fritzl children worked out their demons in group therapy sessions with their mother, in which they all talked of what had gone on and how no one in the family was to blame for what happened except for one individual: Josef Fritzl.

This is the key to healing – smashing the bonds that shackle the minds of captives to their jailer. It is what must happen in order to set the Cleveland women free to enjoy what is left of their lives.

A vital key to the Fritzl children's therapy was operating on the 'slow time' that they had experienced while in captivity, and so it will be for the Cleveland quartet. Too much therapy too quickly can, say their doctors, be as harmful as none at all.

'There will be plenty of time for them in the future to

adjust to the frenetic pace of life as it is lived by most people in America,' said one doctor. 'At the moment, we are taking things as slowly as we can because that is what is best for them. They are just getting to know their families again, their neighbourhoods, old friends, once-familiar places grown strange. As the weeks pass, we can speed up the pace of things to accommodate them. They are in the driving seat now and it is important for them to realize that. Life is no longer dictated by the whim of a cruel and sexually omnipotent jailer.'

If the examples of the Fritzl incest children are anything to go by, there is indeed hope. Both Kerstin and Stefan responded amazingly well to therapy sessions in which negative feelings towards their captor were purged. They learned to understand that everything that had befallen them and their beloved mother was out of their remit to control or influence. The thoughts they had entertained, over the years, of ambushing and killing Fritzl as he came into the cellar were, they were told, natural ones. In as much as people who underwent such mental and physical privations can ever be regarded as normal, they are both travelling on the right highway. Kerstin, who loves music and clothes, has a boyfriend and spends her days with a private tutor who teaches her and Stefan. Both are working towards high school diplomas and hope to move out to their own homes when they find work. Stefan, a gentle and introspective soul, has a love of classical literature and an aquarium of tropical fish that is his pride and joy. He dreams of becoming a ship's captain, seeing a world that just a few short years ago was confined to a single, stinking room.

Michelle is undoubtedly the most fragile of all, her brave decision to confront Castro in court notwithstanding, and will require the most care. Those close to the case say she is shell-shocked, numb, but does have a burning mission: to win back custody of her child. And she has acquired a deep faith in God during her years in captivity. A slow reader, she memorized huge tracts of the Bible in Seymour Avenue and believes God is on her side in her quest to regain Joey. This quest gives her hope, and the doctors believe that with purpose will come healing. She has to surmount the crushing feeling that she was somehow responsible for what happened to her, that she 'brought it on herself' and that she deserved no better.

Baffling though it may seem to people who can only look in on such cases from the outside, feelings of self-loathing are by no means rare. These are classic guilt symptoms of kidnap survivors. To a greater or lesser extent they are the emotions of all three of Castro's captives and will have to be worked out of the women as fresh injections of self-esteem, confidence and strength are pumped in.

Dr Gillian Butler, a consultant clinical psychologist and a fellow of the British Psychological Society, who practises in the Oxfordshire Mental Healthcare Trust, routinely visits people in hospitals recovering from horrific abuse. She told the author there is no 'one size fits all' solution, and that even the experience of the Fritzl and Kampusch cases does not mean that what worked for them will necessarily work for these women.

'Everyone is different. The speed of the recovery is hugely individual. It is all about what this ordeal meant to each one of them. They went through a catastrophic event and there is definitely no quick fix for any of them. Certainly there will be feelings of distrust, anger – why did this happen to me? – and self-respect issues. What their experiences in life, with families, were before they were taken will play a part in how effectively they recover.

'We can't know what they think about the kidnapper. It may be that they saw some good in him, acted to please him, thinking that in pleasing him they were making things easier for themselves. Therapy is all about trying to help people in the here and now, to regain their lives and con-trol over their lives. Getting them on this path means finding out what the event – the kidnapping and incar-ceration and mistreatment – meant to them. Drugs can help for sleeplessness, for anxiety, but there is no drug that can give these women their lives back. They have to regain them slowly over time. Building relationships will be difficult, the feeling that the closer they get, the more danger there is. It is a fascinating case and the care for these women will take many years.'

Terri L. Weaver, a professor of psychology at St Louis University and a consultant in long-term kidnapping cases, told the *New York Times* that the presence of the other captives in the Seymour Avenue house may possibly have helped each woman cope.

'My hope would be that they could have provided some degree of support with one another,' Dr Weaver said, 'and that may have aided in their ability to emotionally, and perhaps even physically, cope with the situation.' Dr Weaver believes that the best chance of all for a swift healing lies with Jocelyn. 'There are all types of children in this world that were conceived in violent and traumatic circumstances who come to an understanding of those circumstances and go on to have very happy lives.'

But Dr Weaver, like most therapists, does not believe that the women could have escaped before they did. Such notions are the mindset that results from a desire among people to believe they would never themselves fall victim to a similar fate. 'Rape in conjunction with life-threatening force is very powerful,' Dr Weaver added, 'and it's repeatedly used by men against women.'

The women, ultimately, were under a spell, woven by a brute who backed up threats with brute force. They feared for their lives because they saw what he was capable of. But the day of the breakout saw the kaleidoscope shift and the fragments of their world reform. Castro created life, but he could not bond with Jocelyn in the way that Amanda could. In the end, the fear of failing her daughter, of condemning her to what she herself had endured, led Amanda to make the cry for help to the outside world.

The baby that Castro doted on eventually destroyed him, because she gave all of them hope. Like the judge said, they not only persevered, they prevailed.

The issue of control is, ultimately, the key element to be worked out with the victims. They all had zero control over their circumstances during key phases of their lives. Regaining emotional equilibrium is what must happen before they can move on, can learn to trust men again, can learn to love again. Elisabeth Fritzl, probably the most enduring symbol of a recovering rape victim, has managed to have at least one stable and non-abusive relationship with a man since she came out of the cellar. If she can learn to trust again, anyone can. Once trust is regained in one area – the simple act of walking to a corner shop without the fear of being kidnapped – then it can be regained in others.

Learning to walk before running is, say the experts, what is needed for the Ohio women. Everyone around them should be careful not to put pressure on them in any way. They have experienced more stress in recent years than most people will experience in their entire lives. Some trauma victims will prefer to stay close to home, while others may feel the need to recover as far away as possible. Doctors recommend peaceful environments – the countryside, the seaside, mountains, lakes. It is the reason why so many pricey drug and rehabilitation clinics and mental health centres are built amid naturally beautiful surroundings.

The women are also being encouraged to help other trauma victims. When Natascha Kampusch was freed, her therapists put her into a group of abused women in a bid to show her she was not alone. And the Cleveland survivors have developed coping techniques that may prove invaluable in aiding others who have suffered similar abuse to recover.

*

Just how much they suffered was revealed to the world on
31 July 2013, the day before Castro left the stage for good.
Dr Frank Ochberg, a pioneering psychiatrist in the USA,
was tasked by Cleveland prosecutors to write a report
ahead of Castro's final sentencing. It is a devastating
document, one that bears witness to both the agony and
the bravery of all his victims.

It takes the form of a letter addressed to prosecutor
McGinty. This is it in its entirety, and it goes some way to
explaining why the prosecutor thought Castro should
have received the death penalty.

Dear Mr McGinty:

You have asked me to evaluate the impact of confinement and abuse upon the victims of Ariel Castro.

Based upon material provided by your office, which
includes videos of victim interviews, transcripts and
medical reports, the FBI investigative materials, visits to
the crime scene, the proffer interview of Ariel Castro,
and interviews with people familiar with the case, I reach
these conclusions:

1. Castro hurt each of the three young women that he
captured and confined in ways that create lasting wounds.

A. He terrified them. The body responds to terror long
afterwards with uncontrollable visions, smells, sounds
and sensations. These are called trauma memories and
they are unlike ordinary memory. They come at night in
the form of nightmares. They come in the twilight zone

between falling asleep and awakening. They come in the middle of the day, often when there is a reminder. Trauma survivors call this 'being triggered'. Each young woman sustained many, many traumas. There is some evidence of post-traumatic stress documented in medical records. Often there are delayed effects, coming on after the exhilaration of rescue wears off.

B. He degraded, demeaned and diminished them. Some acts terrify, others degrade. To be bound, gagged, deprived of a toilet – to be treated in a less than human way – causes not only fear, but profound shame and humiliation. When this is done repetitively and relentlessly, it alters a person's sense of self. We have no official diagnosis for this, but we call it complex PTSD. It is the result of victimization over a long period of time, or in the years when personality and character are being formed, or both. Repetitive rape combined with captivity are crimes that terrify and degrade.

I saw ample evidence of this.

C. He deprived them of ten years of normalcy during the stages of life when a girl becomes a woman, when we learn how to become intimate – to trust a trustworthy person. He deprived them of access to family, friends, school, work, community and country. These are profound losses and difficult to reconstruct. One may appear joyful at the return to freedom and to others who care deeply. That joy is wonderful to see and a good sign. But there is a lot of reconstructive work to be done before these survivors are really free, really able to judge who is an exploiter and who is a reliable friend.

D. He did additional damage, through beating, starving, impregnating and aborting. He fathered a child in a prison of his construction and promoted a delusion that this was a love child. He turned truth and common sense on its head and he fed that to his captives. They are in various stages of emerging from his false beliefs which he attempted to foist upon them.

E. He appeared to be evolving in an ever more dangerous direction, capturing younger and younger women, telling his captives he was hunting for replacements. And what would happen to them if he did capture new slaves? They felt, at times, that they would be replaced and freed. At some level of consciousness, they must have known that freedom was not an option and replacement meant death.

2. Each of his captives, including Jocelyn, the child, demonstrated remarkable qualities and they should inspire us all. First, there is Michelle. She suffered the longest and the most severely. But it was Michelle who served as doctor, nurse, midwife and pediatrician during the birth of Jocelyn. She breathed life into that infant when she wasn't breathing. She coached Amanda through labour and birth in 'primitive' conditions. At other times, she interceded when Castro sought to abuse Gina, interposing herself and absorbing physical and sexual trauma.

3. But each survivor had a will to prevail and used that will to live through the long ordeal. Amanda kept a journal with almost every entry addressed to her mother, first when her mother was alive and frantically looking for her missing daughter. Later Amanda wrote to her mother in heaven, seeking to soothe her mother as she prayed for her own deliverance and the health of her little girl. On rare occasions, all four captives were allowed to be together and they managed to share faith and friendship. Home schooling and instruction in honorable values came from Amanda to Jocelyn and this was endorsed, when possible, by Gina and Michelle.

This is the good news, and it is very good, indeed. But it does not in any way paint a rosy picture for normalcy or a quick recovery. Grave damage has been done.

4. The Stockholm does apply, in part, as an explanation for the young women's compliance with Castro. The Stockholm is named for an infamous case in Sweden when a bank teller held hostage for less than a week became bonded to her captor who held her in a bank vault. Here's how it works. First, you are suddenly captured by a stranger who convinces you that you will be killed if you resist. You are shocked, scared and unable to do anything without his permission. You cannot walk, talk, eat or use a toilet. But then, little by little, you are allowed 'the gifts of life'. You are like an infant, totally dependent on your mother for survival. As you receive these gifts of life, without consciously realizing what is occurring, you feel some warmth – even love – towards

that giver of life. You deny (again, unconsciously) that this is the very same person who has placed your life in jeopardy. You are bonded to your slave master. There are other elements to the Stockholm but that is the one that describes Castro's initial hold over Michelle, Amanda and Gina.

Additionally, they were each isolated and degraded. In those conditions, many will become enslaved. Depression can sap your will and energy. Rational calculation of risk to self and risk to others can keep a person in an abusive relationship. 2207 Seymour Street is now an infamous address. How many homes are there across America where a tyrant keeps his battered wife and sexually abused children under emotional bondage? Experts in my field know many older sisters who feared for their young sisters should they leave the tyrant's home. So they stay.

I do not have enough facts to fully explain why these captives did not attempt to escape until a decade after capture. But I know this. They came out alive. They came out when they could come out.

They acted with fortitude, courage and grace. We have reason to be proud of them and to be inspired by them.

The video came unexpectedly, and was all the more powerful for that. Three weeks before their tormentor was caged for ever, a public relations firm called Hennes Paynter Communications released a three-and-a-half-minute tape showing all three women thanking the public for

their support and for donations received into the Cleveland Courage Fund, which exists to help them build a new
life. The women looked remarkably well – except, perhaps, for Michelle, whose jaw looked slack and misshapen,
probably a result of the beatings she received in custody.
It was an uplifting, inspiring tribute to them even as they
paid tribute to others who have shown such support since
they regained their freedom.

First on was Amanda, two studs above her left eye and
gold chains around her neck, reading from a prepared
statement: 'First and foremost, I want everyone to know
how happy I am to be home with my family and my
friends. It's been unbelievable. I want to thank everyone
who has helped me and my family through this entire
ordeal. Everyone who has been here to support us has
been a blessing; to have such an outpouring of love and
kindness. I'm getting stronger each day and having my
privacy has helped immensely. I ask that everyone continue to respect our privacy and give us time to have a
normal life.'

Then the vice president of Hennes Paynter Communications, Howard Fencl, spoke to Gina, who was looking
demure, sporting a new bob haircut and pretty lilac
eyeshadow.

'Gina, if you could say something to each and every
person out there who contributed money to your fund to
help you, what would you say to them?'

Gina answered, 'I would say thank you for the support.'

Then Gina's father, Felix, cut in to say, 'I'd like to thank
everybody who donated to the Courage Fund for these

girls. I'd also like to thank the family for having so much passion and faith and strength to go along with us.'

Gina's mother, Nancy Ruiz, then added, 'I would like, personally, to thank the Courage Fund, everybody in general and I'm also saying my community, my neighbours. Every single one, they know who they are. Awesome. So people – I'm talking not just people, but parents – in general that does have a loved one missing, please do me one big favour. Count on your neighbours. Don't be afraid to ask for the help because help is available.'

Michelle wore a white dress, an orange cardigan and sported dark-framed reading glasses. She seemed to have trouble reading her statement but seemed determined to let the world know she, not Castro, is the winner out of all this.

She said, 'Thank you, everyone, for your love, support and donations, which help me build a brand-new life. I just want everyone to know I'm doing just fine. I may have been through hell and back, but I am strong enough to walk through hell with a smile on my face and with my head held high and my feet firmly on the ground. Walking hand-to-hand with my best friend, I will not let the situation define who I am. I will define the situation. I don't want to be consumed by hatred. With that being said, we need to take a leap of faith and know that God is in control. We have been hurt by people, but we need to rely on God as being the judge. God has a plan for all of us. The plan that He gave me was to help others that have been in same situations I have been in. To know there is someone out there to lean on and talk to. I am in control of my own destiny with the guidance of God. I have no problems expressing how I feel inside. Be positive; learn that it is more important to give than to receive. Thank you for all your prayers. I'm looking forward to my brand-new life. Thank you.'

It is not only the women themselves who need time to heal. America's Puerto Rican communities feel red-raw at the negative imagery that has become attached to them because of the actions of one individual who hailed from their island. In Cleveland, community leaders continued to express concern that the crimes might be indelibly linked to the city's growing Hispanic and Puerto Rican minority.

José Feliciano, chairman of the Hispanic Roundtable, which works to promote economic development, education and empowerment of the Puerto Rican and Hispanic community in Cleveland, condemned the alleged crimes. 'He makes my life and the life of a lot of other people working on integration issues harder.' Feliciano said his community's marginalization was evidenced by the fact that not a single one of Cleveland's nineteen council members were Hispanic, despite them making up 10 per cent of the population.

Ariel Castro's crime spree will not make things easier. A trawl of internet blogging sites in the days and weeks after the case blew wide open showed a deluge of invective and hatred directed towards people from Puerto Rico, as the community feared. When it was all over, there was a flurry of meetings held by citizens with the words 'never again' upon their lips, the bulk of the audiences made up of Hispanic citizens.

A panel of city, county, state and federal officials con-vened in the church at the corner of Seymour Avenue – the church where the perpetrator had once prayed so con-vincingly for the missing. They came to hear about fear in the shadows: street lights that never got fixed; abandoned buildings where the homeless lurked; the lack of security cameras outside schools and youth clubs. Only one man, named Henry Senyak, asked why a house with boarded-up windows like Castro's did not raise a red flag with locals. Those who lived in Seymour could not answer him. But in their silence was an understanding that, maybe, things could have been different. To that end, the panel of wor-thies who met with the local people urged them to 'get involved' – to get to know their neighbours, even if they didn't love them.

Afterwards, Pastor Omar Medina led a candlelit vigil on the street outside the church where he reminded those present of a 'moral obligation to look after each other. Remember God's command to love your neighbour as yourself. Help heal each other through your faith in God. There was a miracle that brought these young women to safety. Do not lose hope. As hopeless as things may seem, there is always hope. All things are possible with God. I ask you to vow that we will become our brothers' and sisters' keepers. We will not allow this to happen in our community again.'

Geraldo Rivera, America's most high-profile Latin American TV reporter, a veteran of news and talk shows, summed up the fears of a backlash in an eloquent piece he penned for *Fox News*:

> The initial reports of the crime were hideous and unbeliev-able, three teenage sex slaves held shackled and imprisoned apparently by three grubby, seedy, horribly abusive middle-aged brothers. The kidnapping and decade-long captivity of those young women in a boarded-up hell house in Cleveland is bad enough. How could they rob those girls of their freedom, their youth and this substan-tial hunk of their lives? When it became clear that only one of the three Castro brothers was involved, the crime became more emotionally manageable; still, the selfish sadism involved was heartbreaking and outrageous. The fact that a six-year-old child was born in that house of horrors aggravated the terrible crime. The cruel bastard. Did 52-year-old Ariel Castro allow the child a doctor's care? She was born in a plastic tub in that revolting, filthy house. Were there other babies born there, as reports sug-gest? If so, where are they? Did he murder them? Were there other teenage girls snatched by Castro who did not survive to be liberated? How could no one notice either the house of horrors or the monster's sick world?
>
> Every time Castro's picture is shown, ugly and dishev-eled, I cringe. His admitted cruelty will fuel the negative stereotypes and clichés about Latinos, and for a time even add fuel to efforts to derail progress we have made on many important issues, including immigration. As the wretched extent of Cleveland's notorious crime becomes known, there will be necessary scrutiny of the heartless,

wicked perpetrator. And from my point of view, making Ariel Castro's terrible crimes even harder to bear is the fact that he is Puerto Rican.

When I was growing up in Brooklyn and later on Long Island in the 1950s, my dad Cruz Rivera was far more sensitive than I am. Hard-working and focused on our assimilation into our mostly Italian and Irish working-class community, all he wanted was for us to be regarded as Americans. I remember clearly that whenever there was a notorious crime reported, he would say a little prayer: 'Please God let it not be committed by a Puerto Rican.' His reasoning was simple. During that period a half century ago, many Puerto Ricans were recent arrivals having a hard time fitting in. Yes, they were American citizens, but they were still strangers in a strange land, often with English-language difficulties, poverty and worse. And my dad's thinking was that every time one from our community did wrong, it added another hurdle we had to jump to become 'real' Americans, accepted as equals by our neighbors.

Fifty years later, I know intellectually that the ethnic background of criminals should not reflect on anyone other than the criminals themselves. Every barrel has its rotten apples. But it does matter to me. In the same way I celebrated the ascendancy of Justice Sonia Sotomayor, the pride of Puerto Ricans, to the US Supreme Court, I grieve that the Cleveland cretin who did this to those young girls hails from our beloved Isla del Encanto, specifically Yauco, Puerto Rico. [. . .] Thursday morning on my nationally syndicated radio show I started getting the calls. Some guy named Mark from the Florida Panhandle calling to taunt me, 'Well, how about all those hard-working immigrants you're always talking about now? Ha ha.' My sidekick on the radio show, Noam Laden, thinks I'm far too sensitive. 'It didn't even occur to me that Castro was Puerto Rican until you mentioned it,' he told me on the radio show as we watched charges being dropped against two of the three brothers, and the fiend Ariel Castro being held on an unmakeable $8 million dollars bail. 'And even then I was surprised by your sensitivity. I think we're beyond it. Maybe it's generational. People don't look at Puerto Ricans the way they did in the 1970s.'

I hope he is right. I was further reassured by Cleveland's City Prosecutor Victor Perez, who said during Castro's arraignment that he too was born in Puerto Rico. Perez added, 'I want everyone to know that the acts of the defendant are not a reflection of the Puerto Rican community here or in Puerto Rico.' In a perfect world, Mr Perez is right. The young prosecutor is a much more accurate reflection of our striving, law-abiding, hard-working community than the Monster of Cleveland. Still, I wish Castro came from someplace else.

The house where it all happened stood for a time, forlorn and boarded, ready for the wrecking ball and the bulldozer. City officials knew that it could never be sold; the last thing anyone wants is a House of Horror museum on the site, charging the ghoulish five dollars a time for a tour of the rooms where such depravity took place.

Castro cried when he was forced to turn over the deeds to police, when in jail awaiting trial, adding, 'I have so many happy memories of it.'

It is perhaps fitting that the house was swiftly 'executed' – even though its owner would not be. On 8 August a crew of workers tore it down as neighbours and television crews watched and onlookers cheered. Within minutes, the house was reduced to little more than a pile of rubble. Prosecutor McGinty has mooted the possibility of a small park in the area, using the land from number 2207 and the abandoned home next door.

The house was without doubt the main accomplice in the whole macabre plot, a scruffy, anonymous lair that allowed Castro to operate so long without detection. Accusations have flown back and forth since he was captured that the neighbours should have known, the police should have searched his house, something should have set an alarm bell ringing somewhere. In truth, everything is now being scrutinized with hindsight, but during the years when he was raping and beating and torturing, the iron will of Ariel Castro erected a force field around his flimsy home as effective as any electrified fence. His supine, alcoholic brothers never questioned the multitude of locks. His few friends, who already had him pinned down as a strange loner, never wanted to venture beyond the grubby front room or kitchen. His neighbours, ravaged by poverty and burdened by their own daily concerns, had no reason in a street visited over a thousand times by police to think that a terrible inhuman experiment was under way underneath their very noses. A society that likes to boast that it is free and open is thus able to foster pockets of secrecy and darkness.

As it was in Austria, so it was in America.

It was often said to the author during the time I spent in Ohio in the early summer of 2013 that Cleveland Police Department doesn't care too much for the welfare of the poor folk in places like Seymour Avenue, that the PD exists as some kind of super security force for the rich, largely white population in the wealthy suburbs where the roads are never cracked and the nearest thing to a neighbourhood disturbance is a child throwing his baseball on to someone's manicured lawn.

As in all generalizations, there lies some truth in it. The barrio of Seymour, while not exactly a no-go zone, was a zone where police ventured reluctantly, and only then in their insulated cruisers with shotguns racked in the central console and computers linking them to their command centre. These were not community officers but trouble-shooting squads who came to douse the flames of disputes, large and small, before scurrying on to the next flashpoint. The argument, chronicled in an earlier chapter, that a policeman walking his beat might have felt his antennae twitch at the sight of the strange man with multiple food bags, shuttered windows and a child he explained away in different ways to different people, seems a cogent one. It was this disconnect in the 24/7 world that aided and abetted Castro, along with his house. The self-absorption of others was another enabling factor in his ability to stay hidden and harmful.

To be fair to the police, they looked long and hard for

Amanda and Gina, but they score no points in their half-quest for Michelle, someone they wrote off as a runaway because that's what the instruction manual told them to do. But there was nothing in their handbooks to help them counter a predator like Castro, not even how to spot him. That is understandable. The ogres are, sadly, ourselves – they do not come in the guise of Hollywood monsters. They are charmless creeps who hate women as much as they hate themselves. But allied with a visceral cunning, they become the stuff of nightmares.

Self-interest + poverty + apathy x indifference. That is the sum of the parts that aided Ariel Castro to create his terrible world.

He was no criminal mastermind but a cut-price pervert in a low-rent area. Everything about him was squalid and cheap, nasty and violent, dressed up for the outside world as a regular guy. He preyed upon the vulnerable because he knew they were so. With Michelle, he probably calculated before she even stepped into his car that she was someone just waiting to vanish from society's radar, a blip that would pulse for a few weeks and months before pinging into oblivion. With Amanda and Gina, he had inside knowledge of them from his own children, who were unsuspecting and clueless as to the secret world he was planning on building at 2207 Seymour Avenue.

Until we have the ability to detect thought crime, until we are able to read the minds of criminals – like Tom Cruise did in the science-fiction movie *Minority Report* – to detect felonies before they are committed, we have little chance of stopping the myriad other Ariel Castros who are surely among us. Priklopil and Fritzl thrived because of a bourgeois mindset that could not process the possibility these men were anything other than respectable. Castro thrived because working-class people, and many truly poor immigrants, in his world were too busy getting by to really worry about what might have been going on behind the sheeting that covered his windows.

Castro's incarceration was, as much as anything, highly symbolic: life plus 1,000 years. The meaningless rider was meant to imply eternity in jail, forever watching his back, searching his food, waiting for the predators to come to wreak a revenge made more terrible by each passing moment he dwelled on it.

He never found the courage to end his days when master of 2207 Seymour Avenue, but just a month after his sentence the courage he should have channelled to free the women in his grip years ago welled to the surface in his last act on this earth. Ariel Castro, although in isolation because of his sex crimes, knew he would one day have to confront the jailhouse avengers. He decided he could not do it. This fear, coupled with the realization that he would never again see the daughter he fathered with Amanda, fused into a critical mass of despair. During one of the thirty-minute intervals between guards checking on him at the Correctional Reception Center in Orient, Ohio, he hanged himself from a pipe on the wall. Cut down at 9.20 p.m. on the evening of 3 September 2013, he was pronounced dead later the same evening in hospital.

He was not under suicide watch at the time of his

death, and questions will be asked – although few tears will ever be shed for him. Cleveland Mayor Frank Jackson seemed to speak for all when he said his focus was on the continuing recovery of Castro's victims, not on the death of their tormentor.

It is fitting that the women, not Castro, are the focus of remembrance. With his house gone, his possessions gone and the man himself gone, the community continues its soul-searching. Many have turned to religion for succour.

'I hope they heard the bells,' said Evangelical Lutheran Church Pastor Horst Hoyer. 'They, the girls, were held hostage only a few doors down from the church. The bells rang every Sunday morning. I hope the sound of the bells helped them to know of the presence of God's grace and helped to give them the strength to keep going.'

On the first Sunday after the women were freed he asked the congregation to pause, to listen to the bells themselves.

All eyes turned towards the roof. The bells pealed out as tears fell down the cheeks of some of the worshippers.

If only we had known, they thought.

If only.

Acknowledgements

I would like to thank the Prosecutor's Office in Cleveland, police sources — both official and unofficial — and the family of Grimilda Figueroa in helping to make this book possible.